BUSES

YEARBOOK 2023

Edited by ALAN MILLAR

BUSES
YEARBOOK 2023

FRONT COVER: *Cardiff Bus 404, one of 36 electric Yutong E12s delivered to the council-owned fleet late in 2022. These Chinese-built buses are painted in several different route-specific liveries.* MARK LYONS

PREVIOUS PAGE: *Operating the open-top City Sightseeing tour of Chester is Stagecoach Merseyside & South Lancashire 16957 (MX07 BVJ), a Wright Eclipse Gemini-bodied Volvo B9TL new to First. In the distance behind is the Eastgate Clock Tower, said to be the most-photographed clock in England after Big Ben, straddling the city walls where they cross Eastgate. Following pedestrianisation, buses no longer pass under the bridge, but enter Eastgate from Frodsham Street.* JOHN ROBINSON

BACK COVER (UPPER): *On the Maltese island of Gozo in 2003, where the local buses were grey, red and white, was what was this 1956 Maltese-bodied Bedford SB proudly proclaiming itself to be a Leyland Tiger Cub.* GAVIN BOOTH

BACK COVER (LOWER): *TL54 TVL, pictured in March 2005, was one of three Optare Solos delivered to Truronian the previous year for enhanced services in the Camborne, Pool and Redruth area branded as the Trevithick Link.* MARK BAILEY

Published by Key Books
An imprint of Key Publishing Ltd
PO Box 100
Stamford
Lincs PE9 1XQ

www.keypublishing.com

ISBN: 978 1 80282 348 6

Design: SJmagic DESIGN SERVICES, India

Printed in Malta by **Melita Press**
Paola. Pla 3000
Malta. Europe

www.keybuses.com

Highland Omnibuses B44 (XGD 775), a Park Royal-bodied AEC Reliance acquired with part of the MacBraynes business, in Oban in 1972 in the poppy red and peacock blue livery introduced late in 1970. IAIN MACGREGOR

Contrasts and connections

Welcome to this edition of *Buses Yearbook*, the 60th since it first appeared, as *Buses Annual* for 1964. Much has changed since that first edition was published in time for Christmas 1963 when AEC's halfcab Renown was the newest double-decker in town. The *Yearbook* these days is now illustrated largely in colour, but was black and white then, other than the cover jacket. From 12 articles and photo features filling 96 pages then, it has grown to 21 articles over 130 pages, with topics this year ranging from current and recent events to nostalgia and a bit of history.

By happy coincidence, there are some connections between this and the first book. One of the pictures on that first cover was of a Dennis Loline operated by Reading Corporation, then one of around 100 municipal operators forming a colourful part of the British urban fabric. Its successor, a substantially expanded Reading Buses, is one of just eight arm's length municipal operators left today, their stories told by Mark Lyons who observes that six of the eight have begun the transition from diesel to electric power. Cardiff Bus is one of them, and our cover picture this year shows one of its first 36 zero-emission Yutong E12s.

That development would have astonished readers of the first *Annual*, and cheered those who mourned the fact that the previous generation of electric bus, the trolleybus, was fast falling out of fashion in 1963 and would be gone altogether within another ten years.

Cardiff is one of the cities rediscovering electric buses. Its trolleybuses helped kick off Roger Davies's lifelong passion for buses of most kinds. They ran within a spark's distance of where he grew up in the 1950s and 1960s, periods he revisits this year with fond memories of those trolleybuses and the teenage voyages of discovery he made on successive visits to Yorkshire where colourful and characterful — and now long disappeared — municipal operators (two of them with trolleybuses) left a lasting impression.

The postwar products of Leyland featured prominently in the first *Annual*, with major articles on the products it built for the home market and on some of the great many that it exported across the world, with a particular focus on Leylands in Norway and South Africa. The company was very much on the rise then and must have seemed unassailable.

It is but a memory today, but three of this year's photo features are devoted to vehicles from its final decade, the 1980s. Tony Wilson has focused his lens on the Tiger, with due acknowledgment of previous bearers of the same model name. And Geoff Mills and Billy Nicol — contributors to past *Yearbooks* making a welcome return this year — show examples of two of Leyland's less common coaches, the Royal Tiger Doyen and the commuter service Olympian double-decker.

Besides the authors and photographers credited along with their work, two other contributors deserve special mention for the skills they have again deployed to restore and enhance some of the photographs this year: Mike Eyre for those accompanying Roger Davies's article and Peter Rowlands who, in addition to penning and illustrating his account of taking tentative first steps into bus photography, has also worked his magic on several in other articles.

I hope you enjoy all the contents of the pages that follow and that they entertain as well as inform you about the rich heritage and modern day world of buses and coaches. ■

Alan Millar

The civic eight

Municipal bus operation has contracted to eight arm's length companies in Scotland, England and Wales, but as **MARK LYONS** explains, all of them have expanded beyond their local confines and several are committed to reintroducing zero-emission technology

Blackpool Transport has invested in new Alexander Dennis double- and single-deckers since 2016. This is one of its 2017 delivery of the Enviro400 City, passing the Little Marton windmill. All pictures by MARK LYONS

Municipal bus operations, once a defining feature of 100 cities, towns and local council areas, have declined over the past half century to the point where, in mid-2022, there were just eight with around 1,900 vehicles in total. Sixty years ago, Birmingham City Transport (the largest at the time) alone owned over 1,700 and the sector as a whole had nearly 20,000.

Between 1969 and 1974, 34 of them disappeared into the seven passenger transport executives (PTEs) created in major conurbations, six in England and one in Scotland, while four were merged with neighbours when local government was restructured in England and Wales in 1974.

The Luton, Exeter, Belfast, Douglas (Isle of Man) and Waveney (Lowestoft) operations were sold into state-ownership and the East Staffordshire (Burton upon Trent) undertaking was absorbed into the independent Stevensons of Uttoxeter business in a share exchange deal that gave the council a financial stake in Stevensons.

Of the 48 still operating in October 1986 when bus services outside London were deregulated, 46 were transformed into arm's length companies owned by their council and required to operate commercially.

Thirty-eight of them have either ceased trading or been sold to other operators since 1988, leaving — from north to south-west — Lothian, Blackpool, Warrington, Nottingham, Ipswich, Reading, Newport and Cardiff.

This is largely a story of the survival of the fittest, as most of the eight have won multiple awards for the quality of service they provide and their ability to innovate.

All originally operated trams (two still do), four of them (Nottingham, Ipswich, Reading and Cardiff) once ran trolleybuses and seven of the eight have either adopted or have committed to adopt ultra-low or zero-emission technology in place of diesel. All have expanded beyond the boundaries of their home towns.

Sole Scottish survivor

By some margin, the largest is Lothian Buses, serving Edinburgh — Scotland's capital — and much of its hinterland with over 700 buses.

Unusually, Edinburgh Corporation owned motorbuses before it had any trams. They arrived in 1914 and were used only briefly before World War One intervened, operated on the corporation's behalf by the Edinburgh Street Tramways Company, whose lease expired in 1919. The corporation took over the tram system that year and reintroduced motorbuses. The neighbouring burgh of Leith was absorbed into Edinburgh the following year, along with its trams which had been in municipal ownership since 1904. The tram system closed in 1956.

The undertaking was renamed Lothian Region Transport when Scottish local government was restructured in 1975 and the three surviving municipal fleets were transferred to top-tier regional councils.

The regions were abolished in 1996, replaced by smaller single-tier councils, four of which shared ownership of the bus company, which later was renamed Lothian Buses. Today the City of Edinburgh Council (through Transport for Edinburgh) owns 91%, Midlothian Council 5%, East Lothian Council 3% and West Lothian Council 1%. The company was renamed Lothian Buses in 2000.

Edinburgh Trams, also owned by Transport for Edinburgh, has linked the city centre and airport (mainly on reserved track) since 2014 and the line is now being extended into the north of the city.

The traditional Edinburgh livery, continued by Lothian Region, was a dark red called madder with near equal areas of white relief plus gold lining. The current Lothian Buses livery is a modern take on the original, with a subtly different red called weinrot (German for wine red). There also are blue liveries for Airlink and Skylink services to Edinburgh Airport. The trams are white and red.

Ten city routes extend into parts of Midlothian and East Lothian served by the Scottish Bus Group (SBG) before deregulation. Two subsidiary companies have extended Lothian's reach farther beyond the city boundary, mainly to replace services given up by First. East Coast Buses links Edinburgh with East Lothian, while Lothian Country Buses has established routes in West Lothian (including Livingston new town) and South Queensferry just inside the city's western boundary. They share a green and white version of the livery, green having been the colour of SBG's Eastern Scottish.

The newest single-deckers in the Lothian fleet are 30 MCV EvoRa-bodied Volvo B8RLEs delivered in 2020 and placed in service in 2021. This one is in Musselburgh.

There are two other subsidiaries, Edinburgh Bus Tours operating double-deck sightseeing tours and a coach business called Lothian Motorcoaches.

The regularly replaced fleet is mainly diesel and double-deck, including 78 tri-axle Volvo B8Ls with Alexander Dennis Enviro400XLB bodies which have up to 100 seats. There are ten electric vehicles — six Wright StreetAir single-deckers new in 2017 and four BYD/Alexander Dennis Enviro400EVs delivered in 2021.

Blackpool and Warrington

There used to be 32 municipal operators in north-west England. Today there are just two, Blackpool Transport Services and Warrington Borough Transport, which has traded as Warrington's Own Buses since 2018. Both towns were historically in Lancashire but Warrington became part of Cheshire in 1974.

Blackpool, which has run buses since 1921, is the other municipal with trams, operated on an 11mile largely reserved coastal track between Starr Gate in the south of the town and the separate town of Fleetwood to the north. This was extensively modernised in 2012 and a new town centre branch to Blackpool North railway station is due to open soon. Blackpool's was Britain's first electric street tramway, opened in 1885 and acquired by the corporation in 1892. It was the only one left in the UK between 1962, when the Glasgow system closed, and 1992 when Manchester Metrolink opened.

Buses replaced trams in other parts of the town between 1936 and 1963.

It acquired employee-owned Fylde Borough Transport, trading as Blue Buses, in 1994, taking it back into council ownership. Until it was privatised the previous year, this was the municipal serving neighbouring Lytham St Annes.

Blackpool livery was green and cream on buses and trams from the 1930s but has changed in more recent times. Twelve different colours identified vehicles on key routes from 2001 until a yellow and black livery was introduced across the fleet from 2010.

A grey and pale yellow scheme with Palladium branding began to supersede it in 2015, this being applied to the large number of new Alexander Dennis double- and single-deckers purchased since 2016, aided by favourable finance provided by Blackpool Council. The trams are white and purple.

Funding from the Zero Emission Bus Regional Area (Zebra) scheme will enable the entire fleet to be replaced by 115 battery-electric buses over the three years starting in autumn 2023.

There is a similar story in Warrington, where the council has secured £21.5million of Zebra funding to replace Warrington's Own Buses' current fleet

A Wright Eclipse Gemini 2-bodied Volvo B9TL of Lothian Country leaving Edinburgh city centre on a service into West Lothian. This is one of 50 similar vehicles acquired ex-Metroline and refurbished by Wrightbus before entering service in 2018; they were new in 2011.

with 120 battery-electric vehicles by the end of 2023. It also plans to build a new depot.

The corporation operated electric trams from 1902 to 1935 and introduced its first motorbus in 1913. The arm's length company has fought off competition in the 1990s on its key routes and has expanded to reach the neighbouring towns of Leigh, Altrincham and — with Cheshire Cat-branded buses — Northwich. It also serves Widnes and Runcorn, where it helped provide replacement services when council-owned Halton Transport collapsed in January 2020.

England's largest

Nottingham City Transport (NCT) is England's largest remaining municipal with around 300 vehicles.

It operated Nottingham's original tramway network from 1898 to 1936, introduced motorbuses in 1906 and ran an extensive service of trolleybuses from 1927 to 1966. It acquired the small municipal fleet of the neighbouring West Bridgford Urban District Council in 1968. The arm's length NCT bought the long-established South Notts Bus Company and its trunk route between Nottingham and Loughborough in 1991 and followed that six years later with minibus operator Pathfinder (Newark).

Trams returned to Nottingham in March 2004 with the opening of the first section of the Nottingham Express Transit (NET) system which includes city centre street running. Three years earlier, in preparation for this, French transport group Transdev acquired an 18% stake in NCT, which along with Transdev was part of the Arrow Light Rail consortium awarded the initial operating contract for NET.

Arrow's involvement in the tramway ended in 2011 but Transdev retains its stake in NCT and has purchased or borrowed some of NCT's surplus buses for its fleets in the north of England.

Warrington's Own Buses adopted this Cheshire Cat livery, designed by Best Impressions, for the Alexander Dennis Enviro200 MMCs operated on its services to Altrincham and Northwich.

Nottingham's buses (and trolleybuses) were green for decades, but since 2001 NCT has embraced coloured route branding on its main corridors; those on the Loughborough corridor are dark blue in a nod to the South Notts livery.

Pursuit of cleaner forms of propulsion led to the operation of three Scania OmniLinks with ethanol fuel — the first use of it in UK buses — from 2007 to 2013. Since 2017, it has purchased 130 biogas-fuelled Scania N280UD double-deckers with Alexander Dennis Enviro400 City bodies; government funding helped pay for the first 53.

Zebra funding will replace its entire single-deck fleet – Optare Solo SRs and Alexander Dennis Enviro200s — with 78 battery-electric buses between late 2022 and late 2023, with charging infrastructure installed at their Trent Bridge base.

Ipswich in isolation

Ipswich Buses, the only municipal left in the east of England and with 75 vehicles the smallest of the eight survivors, came close to being part-privatised in 2009 when the council entered into negotiations to sell a stake in the company to the Go-Ahead Group. They were unable to agree terms.

It last bought new vehicles (Enviro200s) in 2016. Recent secondhand purchases have included Scania OmniCity double-deckers from London and 13 Optare Tempo SRs from Trent Barton in 2019; the only other Tempo SRs in the UK are four at Manchester Airport which were built for Australia.

The fleet is all-diesel, but Ipswich Corporation, which acquired the town's tramway in 1901, operated electric trams from 1903 to 1926 and

Nottingham City Transport's services in West Bridgford, which had its own municipal bus undertaking until 1968, are branded as Bridgford Bus. This is a biogas-fuelled Scania N280UDs with Alexander Dennis Enviro400CBG City body.

trolleybuses from 1923 to 1963. There were no motorbuses until 1950.

It expanded into coach operation with the acquisition of JDW Coaches in 1987, but sold what by then was Ipswich Travel five years later. It re-entered the market in 2021 with a new venture called Ipswich Coachlines. Ipswich Buses acquired Carter's Coach Services, a bus operator, in 2016 and operates into Essex on a tendered service linking Ipswich and Colchester via Constable Country.

As in Nottingham, the traditional Ipswich livery was green and cream, changed later to green and white. It has been lime green and purple since 2012.

Expansion in Reading

The only other English arm's length municipal is Reading Transport, based 35miles west of London with a fleet that has grown to around 280 vehicles. It trades today as Reading Buses, Newbury & District and Thames Valley, and since 2004 has used route colours to identify the vehicles on key corridors in Reading.

The corporation took over the town's tram service in 1901, electrified it in 1903 and closed it in 1939. It introduced motorbuses in 1919 but began to replace the trams with trolleybuses from 1936 until motorbuses in turn replaced the last trolleybuses in 1968.

It has expanded by acquiring or replacing other operators' services, starting in 1992 when it acquired the Reading and Newbury operations of

The Bee Line, successor to Alder Valley North, from then owner Q Drive.

Services in Newbury, which included one to Basingstoke, were branded as Newbury Buses until 2011 when operations there were scaled down and the Jet Black-branded Newbury-Reading service was franchised for the next three years to Weavaway, which operated it as part of the Reading Buses network.

In 1998, Reading Transport bought Reading Mainline, established in 1994 by former Reading manager Mike Russell to compete on corridors in the town with ex-London AEC/Park Royal Routemasters on which conductors collected fares. It closed the Mainline operation in July 2000.

Like Lothian, Reading Buses has also expanded to take over territory given up by First, specifically its Berkshire company, successor to The Bee Line. It took over the Reading-Bracknell service in 2015 when the First closed its Bracknell depot, and in January 2018 revived the Thames Valley name — extinguished since the National Bus Company created Alder Valley 46 years earlier — on services replacing First in Slough.

Reading Buses provided a replacement when First abandoned Green Line route 702 between

Ipswich has developed branding for some of its routes, as applied here to one of the 13 Optare Tempo SRs acquired from Trent Barton.

Legoland, Windsor, Slough and London Victoria in late December 2017, taking it back into central London after a gap of over 17 years.

Reading had first operated into the capital when coach services were deregulated in October 1980, teaming up with Southend Transport in an ambitious municipal venture to operate a cross-London commuter and shoppers' service that linked the two towns via Heathrow Airport. Traffic congestion made it difficult to manage and the joint operation ended in 1982, replaced by overlapping services. Reading's route ran to Aldgate in the City of London, Southend's to Heathrow. The Reading-operated service was withdrawn in 2000 but the company continued to operate a Goldline-branded coach business for another nine years.

It took over a Reading-Fleet service from Stagecoach in 2018, along with two TransBus Tridents, but has since curtailed it to terminate at Riseley, short of the Berkshire/Hampshire border.

A contract win from West Berkshire Council took it back on to local services in Newbury in September 2016, branding this part of the business as Kennections after the River Kennet. It purchased Weavaway's Newbury & District business two years later and this brand has replaced Kennections.

It expanded its presence in east Berkshire in March 2019 by acquiring the Bracknell-based Courtney Buses business, which has since been renamed Thames Valley.

Although it has yet to embrace the electric revolution, Reading is no stranger to alternative fuels. It operated a gas-fuelled Optare MetroRider in Newbury in the 1990s and in 2008 took delivery of 14 ethanol-fuelled Scania OmniCity double-deckers, which were subsequently converted to run on diesel fuel. It has had much more success with 57 biogas-fuelled Alexander Dennis-bodied Scania single- and double-deckers purchased between 2013 and 2018, and also had five gas-powered Optare Solos previously operated by Stagecoach in Lincoln.

Government funding led it to be an early adopter of hybrid diesel-electric drivelines, taking 31 Alexander Dennis Enviro400Hs in 2010/11. One of these has been converted to electric power with a Magtec electric drivetrain, but the other 30 have been rebuilt as conventional diesels.

One of Reading Buses' long wheelbase Alexander Dennis Enviro400Hs converted from hybrid to diesel drive.

An Alexander Dennis Enviro200 in Reading Transport's Thames Valley fleet on a service in Bracknell.

The Welsh pair

Cardiff Bus with around 220 vehicles and Newport Bus with 140 have survived the demise since 1989 of the five other municipals in south Wales. The cities are just 15miles apart and a long-standing joint service between their two centres is now the only one between arm's length municipals anywhere in the UK.

The corporation in Cardiff, officially the Welsh capital since 1955, took over the city's trams in 1902 and electrified the service by 1904. It began running motorbuses in 1920, but it was with trolleybuses that it replaced the trams between 1942 and 1950. The last trolleybus ran in 1970.

Newport Corporation acquired a private tramway in 1894, took over its operation in 1901 and electrified it in 1903. Operation of motorbuses began in 1924 and they replaced the last trams in 1937.

Something both operators have in common is their recent investment in electric vehicles, Yutong single-deckers imported from China. Cardiff has 36 of the 12m E12 model, delivered in 2021/22, while Newport received its first in 2020 and by 2022 had 34, a mix of E12 and shorter E10 models.

Cardiff's were its first new buses for five years and it has recently also purchased secondhand vehicles including Mercedes-Benz Citaros from Bus Vannin in the Isle of Man (supplementing similar vehicles

Newport Bus and Cardiff Bus have both bought Yutong electric single-deckers. This is one of the E12s in the Newport fleet.

bought new) and Optare-bodied Scania OmniDekkas from Nottingham City Transport. It retired the last of a fleet of 19 Scania OmniCity bendybuses early in 2022; they were purchased in 2006 for services to Cardiff Bay and the large Ely housing estate.

Cardiff has operated to Newport since 1924 and the two operators have provided it jointly since 1945. Cardiff had a share in the operation of two other long out-of-town services from 1929/30, taking its buses to Merthyr Tydfil until 1971 and to Tredegar until the early 1980s. It continued to participate in a Cardiff-Blackwood route until 2001. Today's network includes services to Penarth and Barry, areas served by the privatised National Welsh until it collapsed in 1992.

Newport Bus has also expanded beyond its traditional operating area with services to Chepstow and Monmouth, and over the Severn into England as it holds the contract to provide TrawsCymru service T7 between its home city and Bristol. Within Newport, it has operated a Fflecsi demand-responsive minibus service for Transport for Wales since 2020.

City of Cardiff Transport, as it was then, changed its livery from crimson and cream to bright orange from 1972; this was relieved by areas of white that altered in subsequent years until 1999 when a new combination of Burges blue (a shade akin to aquamarine), cream and a small area of orange was introduced; it changed again to Burges blue and orange from 2006. Fleet livery since 2021 has been two-tone orange, but most of the Yutongs are in colours specific to the routes that they serve.

Newport livery has evolved from varying proportions of green and cream through similar variations of green and white to one of allover green.

The future

The future for most of the eight looks as promising as it can be for an industry emerging from the shockwaves caused by the Covid-19 pandemic.

While franchising in Greater Manchester may complicate Warrington's Own Buses' operations into that city region, its success — and Blackpool's — in winning Zebra cash for fleet electrification is an apparent endorsement of these operators' future. So too is the Department for Transport's award of funding to Reading, Nottingham and Warrington councils to support Bus Service Improvement Plans as part of the government's National Bus Strategy for England.

There might even be a municipal revival, as both the Scottish and Welsh governments have included powers for local authorities to operate buses in legislation going before the parliaments in Edinburgh and Cardiff. In fact, there already are a few council-owned bus operations that are not arm's length companies, notably in Scotland's Western Isles and Dumfries & Galloway.

During 2019, Glasgow City Council held exploratory talks with FirstGroup about acquiring First Glasgow, but these were abandoned when First decided against selling its UK bus business. Similar thoughts were entertained in Aberdeen. Both of these businesses had once been municipal transport departments. ∎

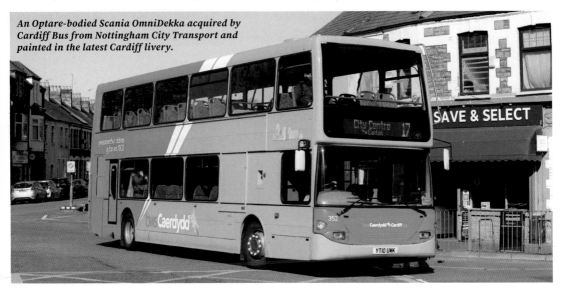

An Optare-bodied Scania OmniDekka acquired by Cardiff Bus from Nottingham City Transport and painted in the latest Cardiff livery.

Deeble & Sons' Leyland Comet MRL 910, with Mashford body, photographed by the late Dr Michael Taylor.

They **shipped** up in **coachbuilding**

Boatbuilders who had prospered in wartime by meeting the needs of the fighting services needed to find new outlets for their skills when hostilities ended. **MIKE FENTON** identifies three that dabbled briefly in the market for bus and coach bodywork

In *Buses Yearbook 2022*, I featured three companies that turned from the production of aircraft to building of bus and coach bodies after World War Two. Here are three boat builders that saw similar potential for themselves as pent-up demand rose for passenger-carrying road vehicles.

All three, hardly surprisingly, were on the coast but in different parts of England: Devon, Cornwall and north Yorkshire. For two years in the 1950s, one of them functioned as a subsidiary of a mainstream bus bodybuilder.

Of and for Devon

Blackmore & Sons, run by Matthew William Blackmore and his sons Harold and Matthew, had relocated within Devon in 1933 from Appledore to the Ford Yard, New Road, Bideford where in December 1938 the firm was incorporated as MW Blackmore & Sons Ltd.

During wartime it constructed Harbour Defence Motor Launches; vessels of Admiralty design and simple construction intended for patrol work in estuarial and coastal waters. Postwar, in addition to building the excursion vessel *Torbay Prince* in 1947 for the Devon Star Shipping Company and converting wartime craft into cabin cruisers, the company built eight bus and coach bodies.

The first, towards the end of 1947, came about when local operator Dick Bond asked if the firm could build him a bus body on an Austin K4/CXB chassis. This, according to the Bond family, was "made up as they went along", which may go some way towards accounting for the unusual appearance of the vehicle, which was registered JDV 944.

Three more Austin K4/CXBs followed, also for Devon operators, but these were coaches. The 26-seat body on the first of these, KTA 191, new in July 1948 to Gardner of South Molton, was of a much improved appearance, albeit with a rather high window line when compared with most other coachbuilders' designs of the time. That was however rectified with the bodying of 29-seaters KOD 719 for Burfitt & Lewis of Ilfracombe in June 1949 and LOD 538 for Ashton of Halwill in July 1950.

Blackmore's bodies on forward control chassis comprised four halfcabs; one a 36-seat rebody of a former Devon General Leyland Lion LT7, plus three 33-seaters built on new Maudslay Marathon III chassis. These were TMG 199, intended originally for Wright Brothers of Hanwell, but which went instead to Northamptonshire operator Abbott of Great Doddington in June 1948, plus NTW 222 and GUY 812, new in August 1948 to Green of Walthamstow and Strain (Royal Motorways) of Redditch, Worcestershire respectively.

Although Blackmore's coachbuilding exploits ended in 1950, the company continued in shipbuilding until wound up at the end of 1962.

The Cornish craftsmen

Sydney Edward Darton Mashford and Samuel Henry Darton Mashford founded the Cornish business of Mashford Brothers around 1923.

It was located then at New Wharf, Saltash but relocated in the early 1930s to the Cremyll Shipyard, Millbrook; both yards were within fairly easy reach of Plymouth. The company's activities increased significantly during World War Two when it built motor torpedo boats, landing craft and motor launches.

Postwar, with work harder to find, it began building coach bodies for operators in Cornwall. The earliest were a couple of 27-seaters on Bedford OB chassis for the Millbrook Steamboat & Trading Company that had on its board Sydney Mashford's eldest son Sydney Junior.

For a company with no previous experience, these were quite presentable vehicles, taking to the roads in June and July 1948 as ECO 746 and ECO 997 respectively. The area of the works that had been set aside for their construction became known as the Bus Shed, from which in September 1948 came

The Blackmore 20-seat bus body on JDV 944, an Austin K4/CXB new in December 1947 to Bond of Bideford, was a unique design.

LAF 180, a 29-seater of similar design built on an Austin K4/LV lorry chassis for Rowe of Dobwalls.

No coachbuilding appears to have taken place in 1949, but in the following year – by which time it was a limited company – two more bodies were built on bonneted chassis and registered in May 1950. MRL 764 was an Austin K4/SL 29-seater for Hawkey of Wadebridge and MRL 910, a Leyland Comet CPP1 33-seater supplied to Deeble & Son of Upton Cross.

Unusually, another five years then elapsed before the last of the seven Mashford-bodied coaches appeared in the shape of Austin K4/SL 29-seaters URL 838/9. Their bodying had begun in 1950, possibly speculatively, but with ample yacht and boat building work in hand, their construction was put on hold. Then as the weeks, months and years went by, they stood neglected, gathering dust in a corner of the works until sold to Willis (Central Garage) of Bodmin, where in 1955 they were completed and registered as shown.

With these gone the company concentrated solely on boat building until cessation in October 1999.

Salvation for Yorkshire Yacht

The Yorkshire Yacht Building & Engineering Company was registered at Havelock Place, Bridlington on June 14, 1939.

It was formed by Yorkshire businessmen Albert Ernest Hartley, a colliery machinery manufacturer from Sheffield, and Arthur Norman Cooke, a wool merchant from Dewsbury, both of whom were members of the Bridlington-based Royal Yorkshire Yacht Club. War was declared less than three months later, and their originally intended activities were put on hold and vessels built instead for the Admiralty.

The high window line of Blackmore-bodied Maudslay Marathon III model NTW 222 is evident in this photograph taken by Bob Kell when it was with Slater of Ryhope, Co. Durham.

Although it constructed some private craft in the early postwar period, the business was bordering on insolvency and sought help from George Wadsworth, MP for the local Buckrose constituency. He was a native of Halifax, where he had a paint and varnish factory, and he in turn contacted his friend and fellow Halifax resident Donald Holdsworth, head of the Holdsworth & Hanson group of transport companies.

Sensing a new opportunity Wadsworth, along with Donald Holdsworth and his father Charles, bought a controlling interest in Yorkshire Yacht. They intended to build coach bodies, at that time

Mashford-bodied LAF 180 was an Austin K4/LV 29-seater new in September 1948 to Maurice Rowe of Dobwalls, Cornwall.

in short supply, initially for companies in the Holdsworth & Hanson group, one of which was Robinson's of Great Harwood, Lancashire. Indeed, Alan Robinson of that concern helped design the halfcab body that was to be built under the control of works manager JS Lees on Daimler CVD6 chassis supplied by Holdsworth & Hanson.

Meanwhile, the local council, intent on developing light industry in Bridlington, had purchased from Mrs Wright of Bessingby Hall a 10acre site, with a 3acre plot on what would become the Bessingby Industrial Estate taken up in December 1946 by brothers Oliver and Charles Holdsworth's O&C Estates company. They wasted little time in getting their project underway, erecting a 270ft long by 85ft wide building soon after from six ex-Royal Air Force blister hangars laid end-to-end.

Before those premises were completed, coaches were bodied at Yorkshire Yacht's existing premises in Havelock Place, along with with goods bodies built under subcontract to Oswald Tillotson, another Holdsworth & Hanson business. The company was also still producing marine craft, with advertisements for its 37ft Yorkshire Seaman, 26ft Yorkshire Sportsman and 21ft Yorkshire Everyman cruisers continuing to appear in the yachting press until December 1947.

Daimlers in demand

Of the 1947 Daimlers intended for Robinson's, five THE- and HTF-registered examples were diverted to operators in Cheshire, Lancashire and the West Riding of Yorkshire and a sixth went to Vaggs of Knockin Heath, Shropshire as EAW 76.

Another independent, Hart (Beehive Services) of Adwick-le-Street, Doncaster, put Daimler FYG 903 into service in June 1947, followed towards the end of the year by the delivery of Daimlers GWU 831-4, although not all of these found employment immediately. Beehive also had a new Yorkshire Yacht body fitted around the same time to DT 4148, an ex-Doncaster Corporation Dennis Lancet new in 1933 and owned since December 1942.

Following a works visit made by Daimler sales manager WL Drummond, bodies were sold farther afield, with CVD6 model FMJ 44 going to Gordon (Radio Coaches) of Luton in January 1948.

It would, however, have been one of the last of the type invoiced by the Yorkshire Yacht Building & Engineering Company, as later in the month, with 15 bodies completed, the business was renamed the Yorkshire Equipment Company.

HTD 75 was one of the earliest Daimler CVD6s bodied by Yorkshire Yacht, one of two put into service in the summer of 1947 by Robinson's of Great Harwood.

The renamed company produced a further 20 coach bodies of similar style during 1948, followed then by 30 single- and double-deck bus bodies under subcontract to East Lancashire Coachbuilders of Blackburn in 1949 and 1950.

East Lancs took over the Yorkshire Equipment company and renamed it East Lancashire Coach Builders (Bridlington) Ltd in March 1950. It built more than 100 bus bodies under that name before going into liquidation in August 1952. ∎

KNA 876 was one of two AEC Regent IIIs for Maynes of Manchester that the Yorkshire Equipment Company built for East Lancs in 1949. It was in preservation when Iain MacGregor photographed it at the Dunbar Rally in August 1973 but does not appear to survive today.

Cause for celebration

As the 90th anniversary of London Transport approaches, **ALAN MILLAR** looks back at why and how it was created, what is its legacy today and suggests that much of what Transport for London does today actually began 110 years ago

Transport for London and Go-Ahead London General acknowledged their rich heritage by painting Wright New Routemaster LT50 into the General 'rhubarb and custard' livery worn by the original LT1 in 1929, the first of a new generation of six-wheel AEC Renown double-deckers.

As I write this in late June 2022, Transport for London (TfL) has reached an agreement of sorts with central government for another one-month extension of its funding. This is the latest of many patch-up deals — a product of a fractured relationship between a Labour mayor of London and a Conservative government — that stop TfL from making the capital investment commitments it believes are needed for the future.

Given such precarious finances, TfL might also feel unable to mark a huge anniversary coming up on July 1, 2023: the 90th since its predecessor, London Transport, brought all bus, tram and underground railway services together in public ownership. London Transport made a big fuss of its golden jubilee in 1983 and while it would be unfortunate if TfL lets the 90th pass by without much recognition, it perhaps hopes it can let its hair down with centenary parties and commemorative paint in 2033.

Regardless of whether there is a major celebration, the creation of what then was the London Passenger Transport Board was one of the biggest events in the history of British public transport in the 20th century. One that helped shape thinking of how such matters should be organised in other parts of the country.

Without it, love them or loathe them, there might never have been passenger transport authorities and executives — PTAs and PTEs — in seven conurbations outside London. The main-line railways might never have been merged and nationalised, and the company buses in which the railways had shareholdings might have remained in private hands. It was a model of how things could be organised and one that other places often sought to emulate.

Lord Ashfield

An older organisation

There is a powerful argument that, in fact, the 90th and 100th anniversaries have already passed, and that July 1933 was merely another step in the evolution of an organisation that by then had been around for more than 30 years, led for most of that time by the men who steered London Transport through its formative years, a period that hindsight suggests might have been its golden age.

The core around which the new public board was built was Underground Electric Railways of London (UERL), a limited company formed in 1902 to build three tube lines (the start of today's Piccadilly, Northern and Bakerloo lines) and acquire and electrify the sub-surface District line. Its first years were dogged by financial troubles, but it was restructured in 1908 and by the outbreak of World War One had become the dominant public transport operator in Greater London referred to either as the Underground Group or 'the Combine'.

It moved into buses in 1912 by acquiring the main operator, the London General Omnibus Company better known simply as General, and the new company that General had created to design and manufacture its buses (and sell buses and lorries to all comers), the Associated Equipment Company best remembered to this day as AEC.

The UERL started 1913 by acquiring the tube railways that today are the Central line and City branch of the Northern line and before the year was out had added the London United, Metropolitan

Electric and South Metropolitan tram companies. You could say, therefore, that the foundation stones of TfL were firmly in place not 90 but 110 years ago.

The remarkable men who made much of this possible were Albert Stanley who was ennobled later as Lord Ashfield, and Frank Pick. Both were born in England but Stanley's family emigrated to the United States when he was a child and in 1903 he became a manager of a street tramway in New Jersey. He was enticed back to the land of his birth four years later to help manage the struggling UERL and was its managing director from 1910, executive chairman from 1919. Pick trained to be a solicitor before joining the North Eastern Railway at York in 1902 and joined the UERL in 1906, rising to become its traffic officer and then commercial manager. He became managing director in 1928.

Their contrasting personalities complemented one another. Stanley was the extrovert willing to take commercial risks, happy to mix with the powerful of the land and paint the big picture. Pick, who never married, was shy, more of an introvert and a master of detail who knew what he wanted to achieve, and — sometimes to the frustration of those who worked with him — maintained tight control over everything that he oversaw.

Stanley, who was knighted in 1914, was elected a Conservative MP in 1916 and served as the youngest Cabinet minister in Lloyd George's coalition government until 1919 and became the first Baron

Frank Pick

Trolleybuses replaced ex-municipal trams on routes between Woolwich, Bexleyheath and Dartford in 1935. The electric double-deck fleet was built to a London Transport design by different manufacturers. The bus on the left is a class B2 with Leyland chassis and Brush body, while the one on the right is a C1 with AEC chassis and Metro-Cammell body. LONDON TRANSPORT

Ashfield the following year. It says much not just of their different personalities but also of their status in the society of the time that no state honours came Pick's way, no letters after his name other than for his degree in law.

Generating business

Buying the General and the tram companies fitted with Pick's key objective on joining UERL: to generate additional business for the underground lines, especially between the peaks. Buses would feed passengers into stations and take them home again when they returned. Rather than parallel the underground lines, many of their routes were remodelled to radiate from stations (main-line and underground) and between 1912 and 1914 Pick spent many — possibly most — weekends prospecting new bus routes by walking every inch of them to understand what lay there.

He also understood the power of advertising and one of his greatest legacies is the work he commissioned from rising artists for posters that suggested reasons why people might use the buses, trams and trains; enticing visions of leisure pursuits, cultural attractions, sightseeing and shopping. This was not a task to be done in isolation, for he also ensured that they were used to greatest effect by tidying up the appearance of stations so that advertisements and information notices stood out where they had to and were not lost in a mass of conflicting messages.

It led from that that the business should have a corporate look, with a specially commissioned alphabet, and for stations and other buildings to be designed to a high standard that made them easy to navigate, while also establishing them as local landmarks that the public would recognise instantly were both part of a cohesive system and possessed an individual character. Like cinemas, they should entice the public and act as beacons after dark. Each would have an individual character to help people know where were but also a corporate look that made clear it was one part of a much greater whole.

Pick formed a particularly productive partnership with the architect Charles Holden in the design of new stations and other buildings such as bus garages, and took a typically close — some say obsessive — interest in the final points of detail as they were built. In terms of sheer size, Holden's biggest achievement was the UERL's headquarters building at 55 Broadway, above St James's Park station, which went on to be the home of London Transport for decades afterwards.

Moving into public ownership

Post-World War One, the General struggled to provide the bus services the public expected, leading small operators — somewhat pejoratively nicknamed 'pirates' — to enter the market, often on the same sections of route as the General, competition that cut into the UERL's revenue.

This was one of the factors that led Ashfield and the combine to push for more regulation and for the London County Council (LCC), which was the main operator of trams, to argue for public control.

Thus was born London Transport, which in its initial form was in public ownership but not politically controlled and was required to operate commercially without subsidy. It had a monopoly of the provision of all public transport other than main-line railways in a 1,846sq mile area in a 25mile radius of Charing Cross.

The hitherto independent Metropolitan Railway, which also had a share in the operation of the Circle line, was added to the underground network. London Transport — a name first used from May 1934 — also became a substantial operator of trams, with 2,630 cars accumulated from the LCC, the three UERL fleets and nine local authorities (Barking, East Ham, Ilford, Leyton and Walthamstow in east London; Bexley, Croydon, Dartford and Erith in south-east and south London).

Had this been elsewhere in the country, at least some of the nine would have replaced trams with municipal motorbuses or trolleybuses. There were none in London, but there were hundreds of privately-owned ones to be added to the 4,300 that the General and associated companies operated in what became the Central Area and a further fleet of almost 900 in the Country Area and on cross-London Green Line coach services. Country buses were soon painted green.

First to be added to the Central Area were almost 370 operated by Thomas Tilling in close alliance with General from three garages in south London (Bromley, Catford and Croydon), identified to this day by code letters TC, TL and TB, the T being for Tilling. Nearly 280 were acquired compulsorily from independents, more still from 72 operators in the Country Area.

AEC was excluded from the new organisation, floated off as an independent company but with a ten-year contract to supply 90% of London Transport's motorbuses and spare parts. Leyland, which provided most of the remaining 10% and had been a major supplier of buses to the independents, had offered a similar deal in 1931 and two years earlier turned down an approach — allegedly from Ashfield — to merge the two manufacturers into one controlled by Leyland. It took until 1962 for Leyland to acquire its London-based rival. AEC kept an extremely close working relationship with London Transport and went on supplying it with buses, latterly in diminished quantities, until 1972.

One part of bus manufacturing that London Transport retained from 1933 was bodywork, continuing to meet most of its requirements with products of its own design built in the Chiswick Works which also undertook major overhauls. It turned to outside bodybuilding specialists from wartime onwards.

Ashfield and Pick remained in charge of the new organisation, Ashfield as chairman on a salary

RT1, now preserved and part of the London Bus Museum's collection, passing the Cenotaph on Whitehall during a running day on central London route 11 in 2014. Behind it is a postwar RTL on Leyland Titan PD2 chassis. PETER ZABEK

equivalent of over £600,000 today, Pick as vice-chairman and chief executive officer earning the equivalent of £500,000. Military thinking termed all managers as officers, on salaries upwards of £35,000 in today's money.

Five-year plan

London Transport began life with an ambitious five-year investment plan, called a New Works Programme, that ran from 1935 to 1940. The terminology might have been similar, but this was benign by comparison with the five- or ten-year plans of command economies like the Soviet Union or Nazi Germany. This would expand the coverage and capacity of the underground network and begin the replacement of trams with trolleybuses.

London United had begun the latter process on a few routes around Kingston upon Thames in 1931 and took delivery of its 61st vehicle in 1933. By 1940, the fleet had grown to 1,721 — built by both AEC and Leyland, and all but the first 61 with bodywork from commercial manufacturers. Trolleybuses made use of the trams' electric power generation and supply, and confined the statutory requirement to charge cheaper workmen's fares to this part of the system rather than the wider motorbus network. Trolleybuses by 1940 served large parts of east, north and west London, as well as Croydon and Sutton in the south, and in place of the municipal trams in Bexley, Dartford, Erith and Woolwich.

The expectation in 1935 was that a second five-year plan would have completed the process by

The General and London Transport bought 238 of AEC's revolutionary side-engined Q in the 1930s, of which five were double-deckers. The first pair had the entrance ahead of the front wheels, while the last and most innovative of the five was six-wheel Q188, built in 1937 as a 51-seat Green Line coach but used from 1938 as a 50-seat Country Area bus.
JF HIGHAM

removing the remaining trams in south and south-east London by 1945. But maybe not. The economic case in favour of the trolleybus was at best marginal and there were growing objections from people with great influence who considered that overhead wiring disfigured the view on London's more elegant streets.

The appearance of the trolleybus fleet confirmed that the single entity of London Transport was a sum of disparate parts. Like the majority of Central Area motorbuses, all were double-deckers (all but one of them with six wheels) and were painted in the same shades of red and cream. But the distribution of the two colours differed, destination information was displayed differently and not in the same typeface, and there were many other differences of detail. The buildings that housed them were depots rather than garages.

The motorbus fleet continued the process of rapid evolution that the General had undertaken in close partnership with AEC, culminating in 1939 with the RT based on a radically improved AEC Regent and which would form the cornerstone of its postwar fleet renewal.

London Transport commissioned some revolutionary buses at the time — notably the side-engined Q from AEC and underfloor- and rear-engined vehicles from Leyland — but preferred to refine and improve the simpler concept of a bus with its engine in the front alongside the driver in a separate cab, and a body that passengers entered by an open platform at the rear. The RT was the latest iteration of that simple idea in a process that continued postwar with the Routemaster.

As London Transport saw for itself with two double-deckers operated from Harrow Weald from 1934, the side-engined Q was 25 years ahead of trend by providing a layout with the driver and entrance on the front overhang where said driver could supervise boarding and alighting while the conductor collected fares.

It saw no benefit in that at the time and remained sceptical of such ideas until new commercial realities demanded change in the mid-1960s. Had it thought otherwise in the 1930s, the course of bus design — and the execution of the Routemaster — might have been quite different. So also could have been its relationship with manufacturers, as the cupboard of shared operational and engineering experience that produced successive successful designs of buses from 1912 was bare when what was known then as one-man operation came along in the 1960s.

The evolution of the classic London double-decker that began with the pre-World War One B Type ended with the integral construction Routemaster built using aluminium. This is RM1, the 1954 prototype, in the condition in which it entered passenger service in 1956 (beneath trolleybus overhead). The London Transport bulls-eye logo and miniature grille conceal a horizontal radiator that would soon be replaced by a vertical one. LONDON TRANSPORT MUSEUM

There was no shared experience in the development of vehicles for this changed environment. Both parties had to endure around 15 years of painful and expensive disappointment before a measure of mutual happiness returned.

The after story

London Transport was changed many times after the outbreak of war, brought into government control along with the main-line railways for the duration of hostilities, taken into state ownership from 1948 as the London Transport Executive of the British Transport Commission (BTC), then as the London Transport Board when the BTC was abolished in 1963.

It was reconstituted as another London Transport Executive reporting to the Greater London Council from 1970 (but shorn of the country buses and Green Line coaches which remained in state ownership), returned to state ownership in 1984 as London Regional Transport and finally transformed into Transport for London in 2000, reporting to the elected mayor.

The rest of south London never got its trolleybuses, the last trams finally replaced by motorbuses in 1952; within ten years motorbuses had also replaced the trolleybus system that at its peak was the world's largest. The Routemaster, bought initially to replace the trolleybuses, remained an everyday London fixture until 2005.

Today, TfL controls the bus network and sets high standards for it, and with the fleet of 1,000 New Routemasters ordered when the second elected mayor, Boris Johnson, was in charge, is capable of drawing up a tight specification of how a London bus should look and perform. Today it is also well on the way to replacing diesel buses with the trolleybuses' spiritual successor, zero-emission electric vehicles powered for the most part from batteries.

But the transport authority no longer operates buses. Competitive tendering introduced new players to the network from 1985 and the red bus operating companies of what once was London Transport — and UERL before that — were privatised in 1994. Nearly 30 years later they are owned (or likely soon will be in the case of Go-Ahead Group) by companies based ultimately in Australia, Singapore, France, Germany and the Netherlands.

Best not ask what Lord Ashfield and Frank Pick would think of that, but a lot of what they created — both physically and culturally — is still highly visible across London today. ∎

Year of the Tiger

In the first of three photo features about Leylands, **TONY WILSON** pays homage to various generations of Tigers and their Cub and Royal variants, his own fascination for them having begun as a schoolboy in the London suburbs

Dog, Dragon, Goat, Horse, Monkey, Ox, Pig, Rabbit, Rat, Rooster and Snake are 11 of the traditional names defined by the lunar calendar for the Chinese New Year. Based on cycles of the moon and sun they are generally 21 to 51 days behind the internationally-used Gregorian calendar.

The date changes every year, but always falls between January 21 and February 20. During 2022 this fell on February 1 and was named after the 12th animal, the Water Tiger. Apart from the Dennis Dragon and Ace (nicknamed the Pig), no others on the list have a bus connection although I sit to be corrected, apart that is from the Leyland Tiger.

Leyland's big cat family also included the Leopard, Lynx and Panther — and Plaxton has named coach bodies after two of them, but none of these figure in the calendar.

My introduction to Leyland's Tiger was as a callow youth back in the late 1950s with the London Transport TD-class halfcab single-decker based on the Tiger PS1. A batch of these based at Edgware garage drew my attention both audibly and visually, as they transported me to and from school on route

240A (Edgware-Mill Hill East). The morning and afternoon rides were an absolute treat as they roared up and down the hills along the part of route that I travelled. I cannot say that the times in between were such a treat at my then seat of learning. ■

London Transport's TD class comprised 131 Tiger PS1s. The first 31 had Weymann bodies and were new in 1946. TD95 was one of 100 that followed in 1948 with 33-seat bodies built in Norwich by Mann Egerton. It was sold in 1963 and toured Europe including the Soviet Union before being acquired for preservation in 1968. I took this picture of it in April 1991 at Addlestone, Surrey during an event organised by then Cobham (now London) Bus Museum.

Weymann-bodied former Crosville Motor Services Leyland Tiger PS1 KA226 dates from 1950 and was acquired by Cumbria Classic Coaches as a working vehicle. This May 2013 picture shows it entering its home village of Ravenstonedale while operating heritage route 569 across the border to Hawes in North Yorkshire.

Leyland first used the Tiger name on the TS1 single-deck chassis introduced in 1927. This preserved early Tiger is a TS4, one of three new to Wigan Corporation in 1932 with 32-seat rear-entrance Santus bodywork built in the town. It was in Kaber between Brough and Kirkby Stephen in April 2002 during the annual Easter rally when classic buses and coaches provide free rides.

Southdown Motor Services 649 was one of ten integral coaches built by Beadle in Rochester in 1953 with the engines, gearboxes, propshafts and axles from prewar Tiger TS8s. They started out as 26-seat coaches and this one was converted into a 31-seat service bus in 1958. I photographed it in July 1977 when it made an appearance at a bus and coach gathering at the Royal Victoria Country Park at Netley on the shores of the Solent near Southampton.

The lightweight underfloor-engined Tiger Cub was announced in 1952 and remained in production for the UK until 1969. This preserved 1958 PSUC1/2, with 41-seat Burlingham Seagull body, was purchased new by Shropshire-based Whittles of Highley and was at a rally at Newbury Showground in west Berkshire in July 2013. Although the Whittle family no longer owns the business, the Whittle name lives on as part of the Johnsons business based at Henley-in-Arden.

Another 1958 Tiger Cub, this time with Duple Britannia body, and one of the heritage coaches that Alpine Travel operates in its home town of Llandudno. WND 477 was new to Spencer of Manchester, one of the businesses that became part of Shearings, and in May 2001 was roaring away from the stand adjacent to the pier with a full complement of passengers on a scenic run around the Great Orme. Also present from the same operator was a Roe-bodied Guy Otter built in 1954 for Llandudno Urban District Council.

Many Tiger Cubs were built as service buses for major fleets. Trent Motor Traction 163, new in 1961 and photographed six years later in Derby bus station, was a PSUC1/1 with 41-seat Willowbrook body built at Loughborough. This was classed as a dual-purpose vehicle, with high-backed seats suitable for longer distance services, and with coach-style side mouldings to reinforce the effect. A Roe-bodied Daimler CVG6 of Derby City Transport is behind.

The Royal Tiger Cub was a heavy-duty version of the Leopard built mainly for export. Doncaster Corporation was the only home market customer, taking 20 in 1965 and 1968 with 33ft 6in Roe bodies with 45 seats and dual doors. The ten delivered in 1965 were type RTC1/1 and included 43, which has been in preservation since 1988 and is shown here arriving at a gathering in Halifax in May 1994. The Doncaster fleet was absorbed into the new South Yorkshire PTE in 1974 and kept this Royal Tiger Cub in frontline service until 1981, after which it was sold to the South Yorkshire fire service in Rotherham for training exercises.

Leyland revived the Tiger name in 1981 for its new mid-engined coach intended to combat competition from Volvo and other imported chassis. Arriva North East 218 was one of two with Duple 340 bodies supplied new to Maidstone & District for private hire work in 1989. They were used later on that company's Invictaway express services between London, Maidstone and the Medway Towns. Both were transferred to Arriva Northumbria in January 1998 for long distance services north of Newcastle. This was August 2003 when it had arrived at the walled town of Alnwick on a service starting in Berwick-upon-Tweed.

This unique Tiger is a rear-engined RETL11 development vehicle that Leyland built in 1985 in hope of securing an order from Thailand. It has an Eastern Coach Works body (originally with two doors) and a vertical TL11 engine mounted in-line. After use by the Leyland DAF football club, where it gained its Q-prefix registration, it was sold to Co. Durham-based OK Travel which removed the second door and converted it for service bus work. It had moved to TM Travel based at Staveley near Chesterfield in Derbyshire when photographed in the parkland of Chatsworth House in June 2009, and is owned by the North East Bus Preservation Trust.

Rather austere East Lancs bodywork adorned Islwyn Borough Transport's 46, one of three 47-seaters new in 1986. Behind it in Cardiff bus station in July 1998 was another Leyland big cat, a Lynx in the Cardiff Bus fleet.

Eastern National 1002, departing from Stansted Airport in September 1995, was part of a batch of seven Tigers with the bus version of the Duple Dominant body that was new to West Yorkshire PTE in 1983. The PTE's buses were transferred in 1986 to the arm's length Yorkshire Rider company which by 1995 was owned by First, which also owned Eastern National.

The latest refresh of Truronian livery — without any obvious trace of First ownership — uses a lighter shade of green, as on 23652 (481 FPO), a Caetano Levante-bodied Scania K340EB4 new to Whippet Coaches in Cambridgeshire for National Express work. This February 2022 view shows it leaving Plymouth station on GWR rail replacement work to Tiverton Parkway.

A **century** of
Truronian coaches

MARK BAILEY illustrates the story of a Cornish operator that sprang to prominence from the late 1980s and retains its separate identity within First Bus

The name Truronian has been seen on Cornish roads for around 100 years, as records show that by 1923 the Richards family was operating three charabancs as Truronian Cars.

In 1964 the business — by then Truronian Tours — was purchased by Harold Brown and Godfrey Davies, with Brown assuming full control in 1982. In September 1987 it was sold again to three former Western National senior managers who took it forward as Truronian Ltd.

Operation of two local bus services to villages to the south and east of Truro had ceased in 1965 but the acquisition in January 1988 of Flora Motors of Helston brought with it services to the Lizard peninsula. The following month the Truro-Veryan service was taken over from Roseland Motors.

The network grew through Cornwall County Council tendered work and in May 1993 the purchase of CR Williams included the important service between Truro and St Agnes.

A major grant from the Rural Development Commission prompted a significant enhancement to the network in January 1996 with the integration of some of the existing routes into a flagship new T1 service between Perranporth and St Agnes on the north coast, through Truro and Helston to The Lizard on the south coast, and improving connections with the Royal Cornwall Hospital, Cornwall College and the mainline railway station in Truro.

Coach operation continued through private hires, day excursions, holidays and National Express contracts. Another major expansion occurred in 2001 with the opening of the Eden Project and the award of the park-&-ride contract within the huge site, plus connecting services from St Austell railway station and from Falmouth, Truro and Newquay.

FirstGroup acquired the business and its fleet of around 50 buses and 20 coaches in April 2008; Stagecoach and Veolia were rumoured to have also been interested in buying it. The bus fleet and network of 26 routes were integrated into the First Devon & Cornwall operations, with the Truronian name retained for the coaching unit.

Investment in the brand continues today under the management of First South West. In July 2021 the Falmouth-based classic coach hire business of King Harry Coaches was acquired along with two vehicles. A new Truronian Classic sub-brand has been created by Best Impressions to market this and in early 2022 an open-top Northern Counties-bodied Volvo Olympian dating from 1993 was added to the unit. ■

Caetano Algarve-bodied Bedford Venturer YNV C317 GRL was only six months old when pictured in Plymouth's Bretonside bus station in August 1986.

The acquisition in 1988 of Flora Motors included an assortment of double-deckers mainly used on schools work. RNA 220J, a distinctive Mancunian-style Park Royal-bodied Daimler Fleetline, was new to Selnec PTE in 1971 and is seen in Helston in September 1989.

Service 289 from Truro to Portloe and Veryan was taken over from Roseland Motors in February 1988. Pictured departing Truro during the first week of operation is E872 PGL, a Mercedes-Benz 609D with Reeve Burgess bodywork.

To support major improvements to the network in January 1996, five new buses were purchased with grant assistance from the Rural Development Commission. Four were step-entrance Plaxton Pointer-bodied Dennis Darts, including N168 KAF, loading in Helston in July 1996 on the T4 service to Falmouth.

Investment in coaches continued throughout, with the Volvo B10M the chassis of choice. Sporting the standard coach livery in January 2001 was Plaxton Panther-bodied W3 TRU, leaving Plymouth while working a National Express 504 duplicate from Truro to London.

Truronian started the new millennium with a dozen ECW-bodied Bristol VRT/SL3/6LXB double-deckers, many sporting a yellow and black livery for schools work. BKE 857T was new to Maidstone & District in 1979 and was in Truro during the school holidays in August 2001 while on hire to Enterprise Boats of Flushing.

Two new Dennis Dart SLFs with Plaxton Pointer 2 bodywork were purchased in 2001 for services to the newly-opened Eden Project and painted green and silver. Y2 EDN was passing through St Columb Major in August 2001 on Eden Branchline service T10 from Newquay.

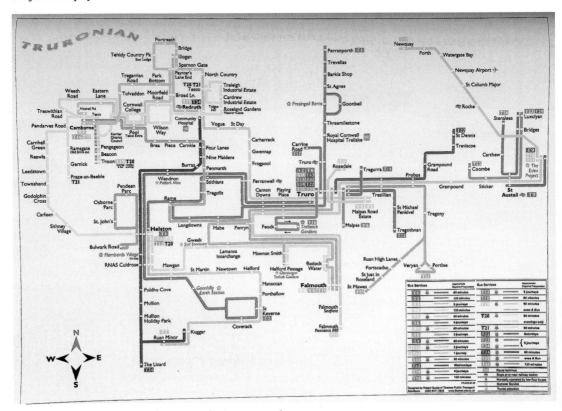

This was the extent of the Truronian network in the summer of 2006.

Plaxton Primo MX06 AEB entered service in overall white before being repainted blue and given Trevithick Link branding. It was only one month old when photographed on Truro city service T5 in July 2006.

Two rare Polish-built Autosan Eagles were purchased for schools work In 2006. These were transferred subsequently to First Hampshire & Dorset but returned in 2018 and were repainted into the dark green used by Great Western Railway, and adopted as the Truronian livery. This is 68301 (MIG 9614), passing through Tregony in May 2021 on the 227 service from Cornwall College to St Mawes.

One of the articles in the first Buses Annual for 1964 described the network of mail bus services in the Highlands, a tradition that Highland Omnibuses upheld with CD13 (CST 961D), a unique 24-seat Alexander-bodied Bedford VAM5 with a large mail compartment at the rear of its Y-type body. This June 1966 picture was taken on the A99 south of Wick on the Caithness coast. IAIN MacGREGOR

Sheer **Highland** variety

The Scottish Bus Group's smallest and northernmost subsidiary had a distinct character of its own, forged by its need to maintain the viability of services in thinly populated rural areas

Highland Omnibuses was the smallest, youngest and most financially challenged of the Scottish Bus Group's pre-1961 subsidiaries.

It came into existence in February 1952 to combine the state-owned British Transport Commission's recent acquisitions in the Highlands. It was built around and took on much of the identity of the Highland Transport Company, to which were added the buses and coaches of Inverness-based Macrae & Dick and BTC-owned Alexander's services in and around Inverness.

In its early years, it was run as a remote offshoot of Scottish Omnibuses in Edinburgh, and supplemented the purchase of modest numbers of new vehicles (mainly coaches) with secondhand buys and mid-life and near end-of-life buses cascaded within SBG. More came through the acquisition of small operators' activities in the 1960s.

The abolition of the BTC at the end of 1962 was followed by the creation of the Scottish Transport Group in 1969 as the umbrella body

The Highland coach fleet was modernised in a quick fix in 1953 by Scottish Omnibuses converting bonneted Bedford chassis to forward control and sending them to Burlingham at Blackpool to be fitted with these new 24-seat bodies based on the Seagull design. Most were 1947 Bedford OB coaches new to Scottish Omnibuses, but C123 (AST 934), photographed in 1962, was one of two wartime OWBs new to Macrae & Dick in 1943 with Duple utility bus bodies. It remained with Highland until 1964.
IAIN MacGREGOR

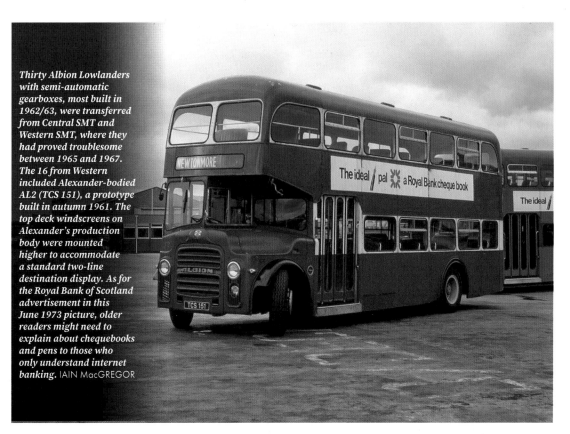

Thirty Albion Lowlanders with semi-automatic gearboxes, most built in 1962/63, were transferred from Central SMT and Western SMT, where they had proved troublesome between 1965 and 1967. The 16 from Western included Alexander-bodied AL2 (TCS 151), a prototype built in autumn 1961. The top deck windscreens on Alexander's production body were mounted higher to accommodate a standard two-line destination display. As for the Royal Bank of Scotland advertisement in this June 1973 picture, older readers might need to explain about chequebooks and pens to those who only understand internet banking. IAIN MacGREGOR

Typical of the near life-expired vehicles cascaded to Highland was JD3 (GCS 222), a 1955 Leyland Titan PD2/20 new to Western SMT in 1955 and operating a local service in Inverness in July 1970, with Highland fleetname and fleetnumber added to its previous operator's livery, complete with dents and seriously chipped paintwork. Vehicles like this would remain for the matter of months until the Certificate of Fitness expired. IAIN MacGREGOR

The acquisition of MacBraynes' buses, which wore a highly distinctive livery of Royal Mail red, apple green and cream, demanded something brighter than Highland's dark red and cream. This was the answer, a combination of poppy red (as used later by the National Bus Company) and peacock blue, accompanied by the continued use of the eagle and garter logo inherited from Highland Transport and set off with grey wheels. Grey was later added to the body colours. AEC Reliance B50 (WGG 636), with Duple (Midland) Donington body, was new to MacBraynes in 1959. This was Fort William in April 1971. IAIN MacGREGOR

for SBG and the west coast shipping services of the Caledonian Steam Packet Company and of David MacBrayne, which also operated buses. Most of MacBraynes' operations were transferred to existing SBG companies, many to Highland in stages in 1970/71 along with the Alexander (Midland) depot at Oban. This led to a radical change of identity.

The Oban services went back to Midland when SBG was restructured from seven to 11 regional bus companies in 1985. The fleet had been reduced to around 140 vehicles when a consortium of Rapsons Coaches and management-owned Scottish Citylink acquired Highland in August 1991 as SBG

was privatised. By the end of the year, it was down to 100 after Stagecoach expanded its presence in Inverness and Cromarty.

The business was split five years later, with Citylink (by then part of National Express Group) owning Highland Country Buses which covered the widest geographical area, while Rapsons retained a smaller rump of the business around Inverness as Highland Bus & Coach. Rapsons reacquired Highland Country in August 1998 and reunited the two parts after NatEx was ordered to sell Citylink as a condition of retaining the ScotRail train franchise. Stagecoach bought Rapsons' bus operations in May 2008. ■

Among the new vehicles that SBG bought for Highland in later years were 18 11.6m Leyland National 2s in 1980/81. N17 (AST 159W), operating a local service in Oban in April 1982, displays the later poppy red and grey livery following banishment of the last traces of peacock blue.
IAIN MacGREGOR

ABOVE: *Privatisation widened the sources of vehicles purchased secondhand. Highland Country B203 (OSR 203R), a Bristol VRT/LL3/6LXB with 85-seat Alexander AL body photographed in Fort William in June 1996, had been new to Tayside in 1975 and was purchased from Lincoln City Transport in 1992. The Leyland National behind also was with Highland Country, which settled on a combination of blue and grey.* IAIN MacGREGOR

ABOVE: *This was the final Highland Country livery of two-tone blue, with eagle but no garter. Volvo B10M-61 164 (MBZ 6454) had begun life in 1985 as a Berkhof-bodied coach with The Kings Ferry in Kent. It came from South Lancs Travel in 2000 with this East Lancs EL2000 bus body built in 1991 and was parked in Bettyhill, Sutherland on the far north coast in June 2006.* ALAN MILLAR

LEFT: *Stagecoach North Scotland repainted Alexander Dennis Enviro400 19041 (SN56 AWO) in the original livery of Highland Omnibuses to mark the 70th anniversary of the company's formation.* DAVID McGEACHAN

This was one of the first bus photographs that Peter Rowlands took in colour, in the summer of 1967 in the French city of Grenoble. He concentrated on the ten-year-old Vetra-Franco-Belge VBF trolleybuses, but in this scene he also captured quintessentially French motorbuses built by Saviem and Chausson.

Before it all **kicked off**

PETER ROWLANDS had a camera from the age of twelve, but for at least a dozen years he took an average of just one bus photograph a year, and felt he had to justify even those. He takes a bewildered look back

If you were to ask me when I started photographing buses in earnest, I would probably tell you 1977. But surely I must have taken at least a few bus pictures before that? I decided to delve back among my scattered archives and see what I could find.

The tiny number amazes me. Between 1962 and 1975 I took roundly a dozen viable bus photographs: an average of under one per year. I can more or less remember taking every single one of them.

What is more, although I describe them now as bus photographs, at the time I saw most of them as "photographs that happen to have a bus in them". Quite different. Back then it never occurred to me to consider myself a bus enthusiast. I never collected bus numbers or bought any bus publications, and none of my friends was a bus enthusiast. I was certainly intrigued by the subject, but I had no inkling that it would eventually provide me with an enduring interest.

This 1928 Guy BTX trolleybus with purpose-built open-top bodywork by Christopher Dodson was fitted with a Commer two-stroke diesel engine after the Hastings system closed in 1959, and was put back to work on tourist duties the following year. It is seen two years later.

In those days I felt I had to justify any picture that had a bus it. I would persuade myself, for instance, that I was capturing a typical street scene, or that the bus in question was quirky in some way.

Go figure.

Summer of '62

It turns out that I took my first ever bus photograph in Hastings in the summer of 1962. The occasion was a family holiday at the adjacent town of St Leonards-on-Sea, of which my abiding memories are the heat of the sun and the sound of Joe Brown's 'Picture of You' trickling from seafront amusement arcades.

In this instance I actually photographed the bus for its own sake. It was the vintage Guy trolleybus known to tourists then and now as *Happy Harold*, and that made it a quirky vehicle, so I felt I had permission. There were no trolleybus wires in sight, and I was already savvy enough to recognise the gruff tones of the Commer two-stroke diesel engine it had been fitted with. It was a genuine curiosity.

The bus is still around, now owned by Hastings Borough Council, but it has aged 60 years since I photographed it (I suppose I must have done the same). As for the camera I used, it may still be in existence too, but I left it lying on a wall in the town a few days later. Oops.

Perhaps not surprisingly, after that I was without a camera for a while. However, I had been equipped with a parental cast-off in time for my next bus photograph, which came a year later in 1963. I was on holiday again with my family, this time at Rimini on Italy's Adriatic coast, and I wanted to photograph the leafy street near our seafront hotel. So why not include that single-deck trolleybus approaching in the distance?

Little did I know then that this was Rimini's only trolleybus line – an 8mile trek between the city and neighbouring Riccione – or that the Fiat in question was already 24 years old. Happily the trolleybus line has survived, though presumably the Fiat has not.

A year passed before I took another bus picture. This one shows a Weymann-bodied Leyland Atlantean in the fleet of my home city operator, Newcastle Transport, and I actually photographed it intentionally in early 1964.

Keeping a darkroom secret

By now I had embarked on a new hobby, developing and printing my own black and white photographs, so I probably drew reassurance from being able to process the film without revealing my covert bus enthusiasm to anyone else. Many is the photographer who must have used this freedom for rather more nefarious purposes.

However, this turned out to be a one-off. My new-found self-sufficiency did nothing to prompt me further into bus photography, and it was two years before I took another bus picture. In the summer of

Built in 1938, this is one of the first of a small batch of Fiat trolleybuses used on the 8mile Rimini-Riccione trolleybus line – then the only one in the city. This is a 1963 view.

The Weymann-bodied Leyland Atlantean of Newcastle Transport in Kenton Road, Gosforth in early 1964. It was new in 1962.

1966 we were on a holiday once again, this time at Kilmory, a delightful spot at the south-western tip of the Isle of Arran in the Firth of Clyde.

When I decided to photograph the hotel where we were staying, I was unable to resist including a passing bus. It looked remarkably antiquated even then; I now know it was a front-engined Albion Victor of local independent Bannatyne Motors, dating from 1951. The bus, I fear, is long gone, but the Lagg Hotel (or just the Lagg, as it is now known) is remarkably unchanged.

In the autumn of that year I made a trip to Cambridge for an interview with one of the colleges as part of my university application, and while I was there I took a couple of photographs in the street nearby. During childhood visits to the city I had been fond of Eastern Counties' Bristol K double-deckers, so what could have been more appropriate than to include a passing KS in the shot? I still feel the illicit thrill to this day.

Before starting at Cambridge, I spent the spring term of 1967 at Grenoble University in southern France, and that is where I took my first bus photographs in colour. I wanted to celebrate the city centre on film, and this time I pointed my camera unashamedly at the buses on the street: twice. Perhaps I felt that being abroad gave me special licence. Both pictures feature ex-Paris trolleybuses. It now strikes me that trolleybuses formed a continuing theme of my early bus pictures, for no apparent reason.

Back in England, and back in black and white, I took my next bus picture in Cambridge's Drummer Street bus station in early 1968. It was one of a series of shots of the city (or so I told myself), and it just happened to feature an ex-London Transport RF single-decker in the fleet of local independent Premier Travel.

Childhood favourites

It was in the summer of that year that I took what is now my most highly prized bus photograph from that entire period. My favourite bus type in my childhood was Newcastle's 1950 batch of AEC Regent IIIs with ECW-lookalike bodywork by local

Passing the Lagg Hotel, Kilmory on the Isle of Arran in summer 1966 is a 1951 Albion Victor of Bannatyne Motors. Bodywork was by Scottish Aviation.

One of five Bristol KS double-deckers delivered to Eastern Counties in 1951, in Trumpington Street, Cambridge in autumn 1966. The culvert next to the kerb, since removed from this stretch, is part of Hobson's Sluice, which dates back to the 16th century.

manufacturer Northern Coachbuilders. Yet in all the years they were in service I took just a single photograph of one. No wonder that shot now has an almost mystical resonance for me.

Looking back, I count myself lucky to have taken it at all. I had switched permanently to colour by then, and had set out that day to photograph street scenes around the city (where have you heard that before?). I found myself down by the Tyne Bridge, and spotted the Regent approaching in the distance. An opportunity, surely? Yet an insistent demon in my head reminded me that photographing it on purpose would be unacceptable.

So I waited until it was relatively close, then fired off a shot that also encompassed other traffic and the towering arch of the bridge itself. Having cleaned and cropped the image, I have managed to extract a passable bus photograph from it, but its existence owes more to luck than intent.

My next bus photograph, taken in the autumn of 1968, was another that "accidentally" included a bus – or rather, a coach. I'd decided to take some more pictures in and around Cambridge, and one of them included a Duple-bodied Bedford SB, which appears to be loading or offloading in King's Parade. It turns out that it belonged to Souls

of Olney, a Milton Keynes operator which, I am delighted to report, is still very much in business. The coach had been new to the company in 1962, though six years later it was looking somewhat dated.

It would be two years before I took my next bus picture. This was something special: an MCI Challenger leaving Cincinnati on an overnight Greyhound service to Detroit – a journey of nearly 300miles. I was working in the city over the summer of 1970 on a student exchange scheme, and had a job as a bellhop at the rather down-at-heel Metropole hotel, not far from the bus station.

It pains me now to reflect that during my entire visit to the US I only photographed that one bus, even though I used buses extensively to travel round the Midwest at the end of my stay. Such a wasted opportunity. Sadly, the wonderful Art Deco bus station in Cincinnati was later demolished, but remarkably the Metropole has survived, and is now an upmarket boutique hotel.

Two Guys in Wolverhampton

Two further years passed before my next bus photograph, if you can call it that. By 1972 I was working in Wolverhampton, and decided to take

By 1967 the mainstays of the Grenoble trolleybus system were 38 ex-Paris vehicles built by Vetra-Franco-Belge VBF in 1957/58. The city then had four trolleybus routes. The system closed in 1999.

An ex-London Transport RF-class AEC Regal IV of Premier Travel waits in Drummer Street bus station, Cambridge in 1968. Beyond it is a Bristol LS of Eastern Counties and part of a Burwell & District double-decker.

An AEC Regent III with Northern Coachbuilders bodywork, one of 40 delivered to Newcastle Transport in 1950, crosses the Tyne into its home city in the summer of 1968.

a few pictures around the town centre. They included a supposedly arty shot taken between the bonnet and the back end of two West Midlands PTE buses.

They were ex-Wolverhampton Guy Arabs, one of them still in its old green livery; but did I take any proper pictures of those rather smart Strachans-bodied Guys? Of course not. As for Wolverhampton's pair of rare Guy Wulfrunians – forget it. I saw them, but did I photograph them?

Jump three years to 1975. That was the last year in which I took just a single bus photograph. It shows one of three Volvo Ailsas that were the first double-deckers acquired new by Tyne & Wear PTE, the successor to Tyneside PTE. The bus was wearing the organisation's short-lived mainly-cream livery. It lasted just five years with the PTE, which subsequently switched to buying MCW Metropolitans and Leyland Atlanteans;

then it moved on to Independent Coachways in Leeds.

Although I date my determined bus photography back to 1977, I limbered up with a handful of pictures in 1976, and for the sake of completeness I should mention what appears to be the first. It shows one of Greater Manchester PTE's magnificent Mancunian double-deckers, in this case a Daimler Fleetline with Park Royal bodywork. It seems I had finally worked out that the only person who needed to give me permission to photograph buses was myself.

Since then I have taken many, many bus photographs: an average of at least 500 a year at the last count, though in my peak years the figure must have been well up in the thousands. Whatever the number, it was a far cry from my apprentice average of just one. There is no zealot more ardent than the convert. ∎

This front-engined Bedford SB coach with Duple Vega bodywork was acquired by Souls of Olney in 1962. It is in King's Parade, Cambridge in 1968, with the Senate House in the background.

ABOVE: *Guy's native American emblem is clearly seen in this 1972 detail of an ex-Wolverhampton Guy Arab double-decker in the West Midlands PTE fleet.*

LEFT: *By 1970 Greyhound owned Motor Coach Industries (MCI), the maker of this Challenger MC-7 three-axle vehicle. Cincinnati's Greyhound bus station, which dated from 1941/42, was later demolished. The massive Hyatt hotel in the background remains.*

Three of these Alexander-bodied Volvo Ailsas were acquired by Tyne & Wear PTE in 1975, but no further orders followed. This one is loading in Newcastle's Blackett Street in December of that year.

The first of many: a photograph showing a Mancunian-style Daimler Fleetline with Park Royal bodywork in central Manchester in April 1976. It had been delivered to the Selnec (South East Lancashire-North East Cheshire) PTE in 1969.

Guildford
The Arriva years

From the perspective of ten years of using its services, **ANDREW BABBS** provides an insight into what Arriva operated in the Surrey town and why it eventually pulled out

Arriva Guildford & West Surrey combined services provided before 1970 by London Transport and Aldershot & District Traction. A&D began in 1906 as the Aldershot & Farnborough Motor Omnibus Company and was renamed in 1912. Arriva commemorated both centenaries by painting the same bus, Plaxton Pointer-bodied Dennis Dart SLF 3088 (P288 FPK) in A&D colours applied Arriva style. This May 2012 view shows it in Bellfields on Guildford town service 3. RICHARD GODFREY

On December 17, 2021, after 24 years as the cathedral and university town's largest bus operator, Arriva relinquished its stewardship of services in Guildford and adjacent areas of West Surrey. Stagecoach South and independents Safeguard Coaches and Falcon stepped in the following day, a Saturday, with replacement services.

These were services I got to know between 2005 and 2015, roughly midway during the Arriva years, when Guildford was my principal place of employment. I travelled to work by bus, mostly on Arriva. When going farther afield, it was by bus that I reached either of the town's railway stations.

Operations were (and still are) based on the Friary bus station. By 2005 this had been in use since November 2, 1980 and was showing its age. It was

the poor relation of the indoor shopping centre to which it was attached and through which access to the buses could be gained.

The waiting areas for all boarding points were under cover and, for buses heading north, south and west, passengers were protected from inclement weather. Bays lining Commercial Road, while provided with a continuous shelter, were more exposed to the elements; these were for services heading east out of the town centre, as the road layout did not permit access in this direction from the bus station exit.

All boarding points had next-bus digital displays along with printed timetables. Arriva maintained an enquiry office with the excellent series of Surrey County Council timetable books in the display racks along with its own timetable leaflets.

Garage and vehicles

Arriva's buses ran out from its garage in Leas Road on the site of the former London Transport/London Country garage. This had a modern maintenance building and offices, constructed in 2002, with six drive-in bays directly in front of the entrance gate, together with a large parking area to the right.

Surrey County Council provided the bus stops in Guildford, mostly to a standard metallic design incorporating a timetable case with up to three timetables of slightly larger than A4 size. The county was responsible for keeping these up-to-date. Thus Arriva's services were advertised at all relevant stops. Stops with shelters were often equipped with next-bus digital displays giving route number, destination and expected arrival time.

In the autumn of 2005, Arriva Guildford & West Surrey had 72 vehicles (there were no coaches) of which 59 were based at Guildford and 13 at Cranleigh. Sixty-nine were single-deckers: 38 Dennis Dart SLFs dating from 1996 to 1999 (36 with Plaxton Pointer bodies, two bodied by East Lancs), 21 Wright Cadet-bodied DAF SB120s built 2002, three step-entrance East Lancs-bodied Dennis Lances from 1996, one Wright Pathfinder-bodied Dennis Lance SLF new 1995, one Wright Eclipse-bodied Volvo B7L of 2002, and the five newest buses, Wright Eclipse Urban-bodied Volvo B7RLEs recently delivered.

The three double-deckers, all at Guildford, were among the last Dennis Dominators built (in 1996) and carried East Lancs step-entrance bodywork

ABOVE: *Leaving a partially flooded Friary bus station in July 2008 on Arriva route 53 to Park Mead, Cranleigh is Surrey County Council 592 (T592 CGT), nominally numbered 3592 by Arriva to whom it was leased. The sawtooth departure bays are to the right.* ANDREW BABBS

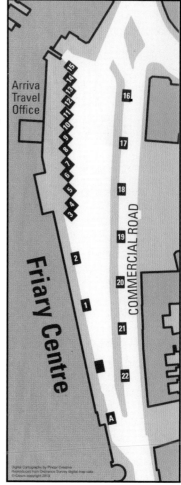

RIGHT: *Plan of Friary bus station.*

The three double-deckers in the fleet in 2005, lowheight East Lancs-bodied Dennis Dominators including 5215 (N715 TPK) filled in often for single-deckers on a variety of routes including, on this occasion in September 2006, on service 436. Behind it in the bus station is a Northern Counties Paladin-bodied Dennis Dart in the Safeguard fleet. ANDREW BABBS

with styling akin to the Alexander R-type. They did little service work, but one service they did run was infrequent town route 6 to the Royal Surrey County Hospital.

Buses built before the Arriva brand was adopted in 1997 emanated from London & Country or associated fleets, many carrying Surrey PK registrations. The B7L had been and still advertised itself as 'Arriva Bus of the future'. It featured several styles of passenger seat and often worked the Arriva timings on route 4 (joint with Safeguard).

Intangible Assets

Arriva ran town services, mostly in loops originating and terminating at Friary bus station, and interurban-cum-rural services extending considerable distances to adjacent population centres. There were park-&-ride corridors to the north (routes 100/101) and south (200) of the town centre.

The interurban-cum-rural routes were in three groups. Heading north to Woking were the 28, 34, 35 and 436, with the 34 and 35 continuing to Camberley and the 436 to Weybridge. Services 25, 40, 42, 44, 53 and 63 ran south to Cranleigh in four different ways by six services; the 25 and 53 reached Ewhurst in opposite directions, while the 63 continued to the West Sussex town of Horsham.

Views of the North Downs could be enjoyed on the 21 and 32 heading east to Dorking, with the 21

leaving the A25 to serve Holmbury St Mary while the main road 32 service continued beyond Dorking to Reigate and Redhill.

Guildford, with a population of 77,000, supported the operation of several town bus services. Most operated commercially with support for some tendered routes. Arriva shared the 3 to Bellfields and 4 to Park Barn with Safeguard. Each operator provided one bus and ran alternate journeys. Four other routes were the sole domain of Arriva.

The numbering of three routes was unusual in employing a route digit – 1, 2 or 3 – with a suffix digit – 6 or 7 – to indicate the direction around the loop. You might think that 6 stood for clockwise and 7 for the reverse, but 6 meant a bus travelling from the Royal Surrey County Hospital via the University of Surrey to town and 7 for town to university and hospital. The north-western loops serving Fairlands and Wood Street were numbered 16 and 17. The northern loop served Queen Elizabeth Park with numbers 26 and 27 while the 36 and 37 ran east to Burpham and Merrow.

The fourth route was plain 18, an out-and-back to town with a one-way perambulation around Onslow village at the far end.

The park-&-ride

Park-&-ride buses had run in Guildford connecting a variety of sites with Friary bus station. By 2005 they linked the Spectrum Leisure Centre as service 100 on weekdays, the Cornhill Insurance car park as service 101 on Saturdays and the purpose-built Artington site as service 200 on weekdays and Saturdays. Arriva operated all three under contract to Surrey County Council using the five Volvo B7RLEs (3731-5), each of which was a different colour with Surrey County oak leaf graphics applied.

Gentle giants they certainly were. I was never sure whether they were governed to accelerate with grace or if the hand-picked drivers were taught to treat them that way. They rolled away gracefully from their stand in the bus station with an air of superiority. Once on the move, however, they had a good turn of speed.

On dry days and when the cross-town 37 was delayed or non-existent, a walk along Parkway – the original A3 Guildford bypass built in the 1930s – to the Spectrum was a pleasant alternative. Here, along with a sturdy number of other commuters, I would await the arrival of our B7RLE. After everyone had squeezed on, the driver eased the bus out to the lights and began the run into town.

The bus lane allowed a speedy run down the gentle Parkway gradient to Stoke Road. The inward run took us up Stoke Road, on into Chertsey Street, with a sharp right at the top to descend North Street. The library stop, served only in this direction, allowed the many folk who alighted a walk downhill to their employment while the bus trundled on to terminate at the bus station. Given the usual gender mix on most bus services, it was good to observe that the 100 was far from a bloke-free zone.

The Artington site is visible from trains heading Portsmouth way as they pass Shalford Junction and that was as close as I had been until taking a lunchtime trip on the 200 during Arriva's last week as operator.

A surprise was awaiting – no magenta (as they had all been re-liveried in 2011) B7RLE was on the stand. Instead, a TransBus ALX400-bodied Volvo B7TL double-decker of which Guildford then had three. So a top deck front seat for the ride over the River Wey, up over the railway – as if you would ever know for it is hidden in a tunnel – then on down to the flatter lands south of the North Downs. A left turn, and Artington is reached with its attractive arboreal planting and central site building. I waited 20min, allowing the B7RLE on the alternate duty to depart before returning to town on the B7TL.

An unusual experience on the park-&-ride and at no marginal cost as travel on Arriva's duties was covered by its Guildford annual season ticket. That was no longer possible once Stagecoach won all park-&-ride work from September 1, 2013.

University and Hospital

The University of Surrey and the Royal Surrey County Hospital were — and still are — substantial establishments generating large numbers of bus passengers. Both have principal bus stops right

The route network stretched considerable distances from Guildford to adjacent population centres such as Woking, Camberley, Dorking, Redhill and, as here in October 2012, to Horsham. Wright Cadet-bodied DAF SB120 3516 (LF52 USZ) was passing through Wonersh on its way south between Guildford and Cranleigh. DAVID HEATH

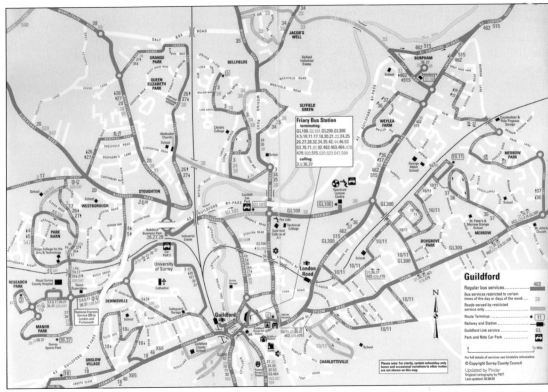

This shows the bus services in Guildford as they were in 2010, following the start of the 36/37 University Loop service with the Surrey Research Park then only traversed by route 3.

outside the main entrances and nearer thereto than any car parks. Each had two stops with waiting shelters situated on a one-way loop, one for buses to town and the other for those going away from town.

Arriva ran every 10min on its 26/36 (to town) and 27/37 (from town), supplemented in both directions by the 3 (half-hourly) and 17 (hourly). With nine buses an hour, Arriva advertised the frequency as 'up to every 7min' on an orange swoop with the university logo on its Pointer Darts. It later removed this rather dubious claim.

The bus route through the university was on its private road network and to avoid the roads being used as a through route by unauthorised vehicles, a bus gate was placed at the town end. Bus drivers had to open their signalling window and swipe a reader with an electronic card to gain access. There was no similar access restriction at the hospital where the loop was shared by buses and emergency ambulances.

Services through the university ran with the permission of the university which ran a tendering process periodically. Given the large number

of staff and students making regular use of the service, the deal included the issue of three-monthly and annual Arriva Guildford season tickets by the university at about a quarter of the full price. Those tickets bore the number of the individual's university ID card and both had to be shown to the driver on boarding. A similar arrangement was available to hospital staff although I believe their discount level was less.

Student sports and loops

A major change in service patterns occurred at the start of the 2010 summer term when the university opened the Surrey Sports Park on the west side of the A3 together with further student accommodation at Manor Park.

To serve these, the 37 was extended from its Gill Avenue terminus anticlockwise through Manor Park to the sports park and then on to terminate back at the university. The 36 now began at the university, ran clockwise via the sports park and Manor Park to then pick up its original route via the hospital back to the university and on to the town centre. This was marketed as the University Loop and provided buses every 10min from the student residences to the university – half via the hospital and half via the sports park.

Chaos reigned as students never knew in which direction the next bus would arrive. So half waited one side of busy Gill Avenue betting on a 36, while the others were at the residences stop, anticipating a 37. Regardless of whichever bus arrived first, there was always a mad dash across the road to jump aboard. Close misses with traffic abounded. This mad, and potentially dangerous, situation lasted two academic years.

In September 2012 the section of the 36/37 via the hospital was removed and all buses served the sports park. But without the loop the service frequency reverted to every 20min to/from Manor Park. That was fine out of term time, but not in term.

Enter route 38, a both directions link University-Sports Park-Manor Park, running over the same roads as the 36/37 and timed to increase overall frequency to every 10min. Arriva brought in a double deck Volvo B7TL from the Medway towns especially for the 38. The 36/37 plus 38 arrangement endured beyond my time in Guildford. But as with the University Loop, there was an unintended consequence. The new double-size bus shelter installed at the Gill Avenue stop was no longer served, so students had to wait under umbrellas in Manor Park.

Fleet renewal

Had Arriva Guildford & West Surrey been a standalone unit, rather than part of Arriva Southern Counties, there would have been an expectation of six new buses a year assuming a 12-year life. One major factor meant that this did not occur over the ten years from 2005: the fleet age profile. There were 28 Darts dating mainly from 1996/97 and 22 DAF SB120s new in 2002.

Fleet renewal occurred when buses were required for contract requirements or when the existing ones were around 15 years old. Many of the incoming buses were not new, but sourced from elsewhere within Arriva and thus partly written down in capital cost terms.

The loss of one of the 2002 DAFs to fire damage was made good with a brand new replacement of the same type, VDL-badged 3970 (YJ06 LFZ) in 2006. Three new Mercedes-Benz Citaros – 3901-3 (BX56 VTU-W) – arrived later the same year in a special blue and silver livery specifically for a revised 436 service serving Mercedes-Benz World at Brooklands from Weybridge.

Although allocated to Guildford, they were rarely seen in service in the town but one evening George, our regular driver, sourced one for our after-work cross-town run to Burpham on the 36. He was in his element, enjoying every moment he had behind the wheel of this well-appointed, spacious and powerful beast. With a twinkle in his eye, he announced to every joining passenger, "Welcome

Before the Wright-bodied Volvo B7RLEs were all repainted deep pink in 2011, they were the fun part of Arriva's Guildford fleet. Each had a different base colour representing a season of the year. Leaving the town for Artington on the 200 in September 2009 sunshine is GN54 MYP which, on paper, was 3732. Fleetnumbers were not carried until the 2011 repaints. ANDREW BABBS

This scene at the railway station bus stop is perhaps too typical of Arriva in Guildford. Plaxton Pointer-bodied Dennis Dart SLF 3401 (R311 NGM), 14 years old, had been cascaded from Southend. It was showing the wrong destination (because old blinds do not evolve like the route network) and the driver is wearing a hi-viz vest. ANDREW BABBS

aboard Arriva's new bus," before giving us one of the best homeward trips we had ever had.

Surprising additions to the Guildford fleet were four step-entrance Mercedes-Benz Vario minibuses, as most single-deck buses in the fleet were low-floor. They had Plaxton Pointer 2 and Alexander ALX100 bodies and appeared on lesser used rural routes and the 802 park-&-ride for Royal Surrey County Hospital staff. This service had started in August 2010 as part of a drive to increase visitor car parking spaces, with non-essential car users leaving their vehicles at Westway park-&-ride site and completing their journey to work by bus.

More typical small buses were two Optare Solos and two TransBus Mini Pointer Darts which took up the contracts to operate Surrey County Council routes 462 and 463. Darts 1606/07 (GN04 UCW/X) and Solo 1507 (YJ57 EKN) were perfectly acceptable vehicles but the state of Solo 1508 (YN03 NCF) was below par, especially the seat upholstery. Not a bus likely to win new passengers or retain existing ones.

Six new buses in 2008 formed the second half of a batch of 12 Alexander Dennis Enviro200s. They were intended for Woking route 91, but that did not stop 4017-22 from appearing regularly on Guildford town routes. The first six, 4011-16, came to Guildford later to replace older Pointer Darts. Arriva informed passengers of their arrival in the September 2012 timetable as "newer vehicles offering greater comfort and improved emissions standards". Two slightly newer Enviro200s, 4044/45, joined them later.

Given the earlier departure for Kent of the Dominators, it was a pleasant surprise when two Volvo B7TLs with TransBus ALX400 bodies moved in the opposite direction, mainly to provide the required capacity for schools work. They were joined in 2012 by a third from the same large 6401-49 batch for new route 38 linking university sites.

Around the Research Park

The Surrey Research Park is an office development in a landscaped setting on the western edge of Guildford. It is owned by the University of Surrey and many of the companies based there have a research bias, often with links to faculties at the university. The research park has a two-way loop road beginning and ending at the same roundabout at the top of Gill Avenue.

In 2005 I found that it was not served by bus, despite the large number of people working there. The nearest stop was in Gill Avenue. Arriva started serving the loop road with morning peak journeys on routes 36/37 in September 2006. Stops were provided at the farthest part of the loop and on the return side but not at the entrance.

Some drivers would stop conveniently on Gill Avenue before the roundabout, to allow folk to alight while others would stop just after the roundabout. Passengers appreciated these unsigned stops. Confusion and annoyance was caused when passengers rang the bell to alight but drivers ignored the requests to stop and journeyed on to the

ABOVE: *For passengers, one of Arriva's best decisions was to invest in Hanover electronic destination displays for most of the town's buses, including Plaxton Pointer-bodied Dennis Dart SLF 3097 (R297 CMV) on circular service 27. The claim of buses every 7min to the university was questionable.*
ANDREW BABBS

RIGHT: *The April 2010 town service timetable showed the correct daytime frequency of buses every 10min to the university.*

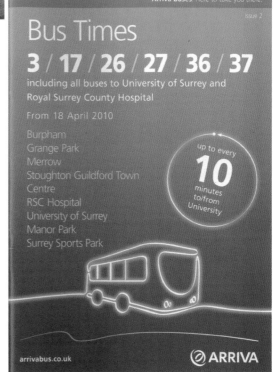

farthest marked stop. Better guidance from Arriva management could have addressed this issue.

The morning peak-only journeys were supplemented by an all-day service on route 3 from January 2007. This route was shared between Arriva and Safeguard on the Bellfields to Friary bus station section, each running every 40min. In a brave move, Arriva extended its between peaks journeys via the university and hospital to run round the Research Park loop.

The links between the Bellfields section up to the hospital seemed admirable and generated some patronage, mostly from passengers who would have taken a 26/27 or 36/37 had they arrived first. But few used it around the Research Park. I used it for lunchtime trips to and from town and often had the bus to myself, driver excepted, and after four years of trying, Arriva threw in the towel. The 3 now ran to Gill Avenue only, except for three morning peak trips around the Research Park loop (replacing the 36/37). Fifteen months later, the 3 retreated from the cross-town extension altogether. So the Research Park lost its buses and researchers had to mix it with students on the 36/37 at the Manor Park bus stop.

Driving staff

The primary observation I would make about Arriva's bus drivers in Guildford was their honesty in fare collection and ticket issuing. There was never any hint of financial impropriety during any of the many trips I made over the ten years.

The varied duty rosters, changing a driver's work schedule day-by-day, was beneficial in this respect.

Drivers signed on and off duty at Leas Road garage. Those taking over a bus during the day made the 5 to 10min walk to the bus station to do so. They carried their duty boxes containing cash tray, ticket machine plug-in module and spare ticket rolls. Their roster was a clear plastic laminated A4 sheet showing bus timings, route number and destination display settings.

How they set about their job appeared to be largely at their own discretion. Inspectors and other supervisory staff at the bus station seemed absent except on special occasions when a driver would volunteer to be bus station inspector. Keeping time during the journey was a driver's responsibility. Most took this seriously and, aside from late running caused by heavy traffic, kept time admirably. If criticism could be made, it would be of early running in the evening on trips towards the bus station.

One odd culture for which I never understood the reason was the wearing of yellow hi-viz vests by some drivers as if this somehow improved safety while they were at the wheel. These were less in evidence on the park-&-ride routes.

Drivers varied in attitude towards passenger loading at the bus station. Some were on their bus before departure time, letting passengers board and pay their fare, while others waited for the advertised time before appearing, consequently leaving late if there was a hefty queue. Rest periods were scheduled to be taken at the bus station where there were meal facilities at concourse level and an upstairs rest room. Much banter could often be heard emanating therefrom

Digital destinations

Arriva did make one investment that benefited passengers using the network, even though it was not in new buses that many would have liked. In 2005, most of the fleet had destination blinds, which were fine for spotting your approaching conveyance during daylight hours, but pretty hopeless after dark.

Many were the occasions when, waiting at a request stop, you either had to signal to every approaching bus or risk putting your arm out too late for the driver to react. Enter, on cue, the digital Hanover display. Arriva equipped all the town fleet of Pointer Darts, as well as others, with these brilliant route indicators.

Clear to see in daylight and in the evening hours, they made life hailing a bus to stop so much easier on a dark wet night when the route number could be read with confidence while the bus was still over 100m away. No more hailing an Abellio 515 when an Arriva 36 was expected.

Of course, this only worked if the display was set correctly. Consider this scenario. Three regulars are waiting at the Boxgrove bus stop for the 07:52 service 37 to town and onwards to the university and hospital. No doubt it is on its way. The digital display tells us so: 10min changed to 7min. A route 36 Arriva passes opposite heading for Burpham. Now our bus is 5min away. It has left Sainsburys, my fellow intending passenger observes. By the 3min mark, it should be doing the Weylea Farm loop.

The display changes to 'Due', meaning it should be no more than 2min until it rounds the slight bend

TransBus Mini Pointer Dart 1630 (LF52 USC) in Reigate in 2015 on route 32. The street sign alongside is for Lesbourne Road, location of the erstwhile London Country Bus Services head office. DAVID JENKINS

Among the Surrey County Council tendered service contracts that Arriva lost in September 2012 was the 25 to Cranleigh, awarded to Buses Excetera. This August 2014 picture shows its Plaxton Mini Pointer-bodied Dennis Dart SLF 580 (S80 ETC), new to Countryliner as RL51 CXC, at Goose Green, Gomshall. The concrete bus stop pole alongside dated back to London Transport times. RICHARD KIRWIN

in London Road and one of us puts out our hand. A stream of cars passes but no bus. Where can it be? The following 37 is shown on screen making steady progress on its outward journey via Merrow.

An Abellio 515 arrives, no use for those of us heading to the far side of town. The display changes. Our 37 scrolls from sight, as does the 515. The next 37 is still 20min off. "Okay," someone remarks,"which car was the Arriva one this morning?"

While such occurrences were infrequent, they did happen. The false display may not have been Arriva's fault, probably being a Surrey County Council system glitch. But the failure to provide a bus as timetabled was Arriva's problem and did not reflect well on the company. Not that those waiting could do much at the time other than make a light hearted joke of it.

Tendered losses and gains

Over the passing years, gradual changes occurred in the variety of bus companies using the bus station, these triggered by the results of bus service tenders issued by Surrey County Council.

Cranleigh garage closed in September 2012 after Arriva lost the contracts for routes 24, 25, 42 and 44 to independents and transferred the 53/63 via Bramley Green to Guildford. That may not have affected Guildford's viability unduly, but worse was to come. On the retender of the park-&-ride services

in September 2013, Stagecoach put in a winning package bid for all four routes with the small exception of the retention by Arriva of the weekend Spectrum work, which was technically not park-&-ride and was on a separate contract.

This loss of prestige work meant that the fixed costs of running Guildford garage had to be carried by a fleet of five fewer buses. One other result was that Stagecoach parked a spare bus for use as the park-&-ride control in Friary bus station, giving it the opportunity to assess other Arriva work that might be added later to its portfolio.

Arriva also made some gains. The staff park-&-ride 802 was one. Another, in September 2011, was the 462/463 (Guildford-Woking via Send) previously operated by Countryliner.

After I left the area in 2015, Arriva lost the university services to Stagecoach and engaged in a bitter battle with Safeguard which resulted in the independent company regaining town route 3 to Bellfields. Thus weakened, Arriva found it increasingly difficult to make its 50-bus unit in Guildford pay, a state made worse by the Covid pandemic. It was little surprise to me that the decision was made to cease operations in the town. My only surprise is that it took so long. ∎

· *Maps reproduced by kind permission of Surrey County Council*

A 1973 Leyland Royal Tiger Worldmaster with Jonckheere bodywork spotted in Verviers in Belgium in 1992, sporting two Leyland badges on the front to dispel any doubts. All pictures by GAVIN BOOTH

Abroad starts at Calais

Beginning with a cross-Channel day trip, **GAVIN BOOTH** has developed a fascination for the buses of continental Europe, savouring both the differences and similarities when comparing them with those back home

For those of us growing up in the 1950s with an interest in buses, but only a limited selection of books to help us, it was easy to believe that buses all over the world were similar to ours – sturdy single-deckers and double-deckers.

We knew that all of ours were built in Britain – in central Scotland, northern England, the West Midlands, London suburbs, the West Country and, intriguingly, seaside resorts scattered around England. We knew that British-built buses were exported to other countries, often members of the British Commonwealth, but we had little opportunity to find out what buses were like in countries beyond our shores, even those in our near neighbours in mainland Europe.

All of that changed as foreign travel became easier and cheaper and families broadened their holiday horizons. My appetite was whetted by a day trip *en famille* from Folkestone to Calais and my first encounter with a different breed of bus, left-hand drive of course, but with more doors than we were

used to, and built by manufacturers we knew little or nothing about. The world – well, mainland Europe – was my oyster.

I gradually built up a portfolio of European countries I have visited – alphabetically Austria, Belgium, Cyprus, Czech Republic, Denmark, France, Germany, Hungary, Italy, Netherlands , Portugal, Spain, Sweden and Switzerland. Cities are my first love and I allowed myself to be distracted by the trams and even trolleybuses that provided the front-line public transport in some cities where the good old motorbus had been relegated to a secondary, mainly suburban role.

Domestic support

Just as we Brits only bought buses built on our shores, it was no surprise to discover that things were much the same in countries that had a thriving bus manufacturing industry, loyally supported by operators, doubtless a result of overt or covert pressure to safeguard local jobs.

As the European Union developed, a new breed of pan-European bus appeared and tendering for the supply of new buses brought unfamiliar types into countries that had been stolidly supporting local industry. Including the UK.

This allowed some of the larger manufacturers to sell well beyond their previously captive markets, so names like DAF, Fiat-owned Iveco, MAN, Mercedes-Benz, Neoplan, Scania, Van Hool and Volvo became much more familiar throughout mainland Europe. And, from the 1970s, they even infiltrated the UK, and though the UK-based manufacturers were having limited success in Europe, this was offset by success in selling double-deckers to the Far East.

So in my European travels I set out to find UK-built buses and the more quirky types that were an antidote to the increasing numbers of highly standardised types that were appearing in many fleets. I succeeded to a degree, sustained by the joys of fascinating places, good food and wine, innovative approaches to bus operation and, yes I confess, trolleybuses and trams.

Even in my advancing years I enjoy the surprises that European operators can spring. Nowadays I could scour the internet for details about what public transport to expect when I reach my European destinations, but where is the fun in that?

Okay, it was difficult not to be aware of the quirky open rear platform Paris buses of yore, or the impressive double-deckers in Berlin or even the sleek trams in Amsterdam, but stepping out of an airport or railway station to be greeted by an array of unfamiliar buses in unfamiliar liveries is still a thrill.

My family and friends think this is slightly sad, and I am occasionally inclined to agree with them, but mostly it marks the start of a holiday. Once we are installed in our accommodation I am straining at the leash to find the tourist information office or, even better, the transport information office; we never hire a car, so the way we sightsee is by public transport, locally on buses and trams and farther afield by rail.

The problem is sometimes working out where the buses actually go, in the absence of maps and, sometimes more difficult, just how to pay for your travel. Do you pay the driver on the bus, or do you need a ticket before you board? And if you need a ticket, where do you buy one?

These days multi-journey and day tickets are widely available and in Budapest it was exciting to discover that senior citizens travel free on production of their passports – a privilege no elderly Scotsman could possibly ignore. Needless to say, many free journeys were made.

Weird and wonderful

There is an understandable move by manufacturers to produce buses that suit all markets, and models like the Mercedes-Benz Citaro and Scania OmniCity seem to be everywhere, including the UK. So I seek out the more unusual types – familiar chassis with unfamiliar bodies, weird and wonderful single-

The aggressive look of a Fiat 421 in Genoa in 1996. Like contemporary Paris buses, the driver was perched above the engine to give a spacious and accessible passenger space.

deckers where the driver sits above the engine, double-deckers of all types including any built in the UK, quirky minibuses. Anything odd, in fact.

And I get really excited – well, as excited as any Scotsman can get – by the discovery of busways in places as varied as Essen, Nantes and Utrecht. And although electric and gas buses are still fairly new in the UK in any quantity, continental manufacturers have been experimenting with them for years.

As I recall, the idea of placing the engine of a bus under the driver's seat originated in France in the mid-1960s as a means of minimising engine intrusion, maximising passenger space and keeping the floor level down. In addition to the inevitable Paris types I also found examples in Italy – Fiats (of course) working for the municipal fleets in Genoa, Milan and Turin. The Genoa buses looked splendidly aggressive, the Milan ones had more than a *soupçon* of their Parisian counterparts, while the Turin ones were just weird and ungainly – but all were fascinating to see and travel on.

Continental minibuses and midibuses have always intrigued me. Some are deliberately small enough to penetrate narrow city centre alleyways that are often otherwise pedestrian-only.

The midibuses sometimes turn out to be slightly shrunken versions of full-size heavyweight single-deckers, expensive to buy and run but allowing standardisation in heavily-subsidised fleets. So

it was a pleasant surprise to find Dennis Darts in Madrid, the model that was hugely successful in the UK market because it was cheaper to buy and run.

Impressive busways

The idea that buses deserve their own space to manoeuvre through traffic more quickly and easily is not a new one. In the UK we have had bus lanes for decades now and there are several excellent examples of segregated busways that give buses priority through anything from an awkward junction to substantial portions of a busy route.

So it is in mainland Europe. The Dutch offer several examples, from the stretches of busway in Utrecht that were served on my 2004 visit by impressive double-articulated Van Hool AGG300s to the ambitious Zuidtangent scheme introduced in 2002, initially linking a suburban station in Amsterdam with Schiphol Airport and the town of Haarlem.

It uses roads and motorways between Amsterdam and Schiphol, with bus priority at crossings, but for the remaining 25km to Haarlem it has its own dedicated busway, complete with tram-style stops. When it was first introduced it was suggested that if traffic reached the right levels it could become an interurban tramway.

The same principle applied in France with the segregated busway (catchily named BusWay) in Nantes, a city that already has a busy tramway. Here in 2006 a 7km busway was introduced, linked

One of 11 Dennis Dart SLFs with Spanish-built Unvi Cidade bodies built for Autobuses Prisei of Madrid between 2000 and 2007 – this is the first example, delivered early in 2000.

The Essen guided busway in 1993 with a Mercedes-Benz O305G picking up at one of the stops located between the carriageways of a busy road.

Allegedly, somewhere under this splendid beast photographed in Valletta, Malta in 2003 is a former Lincolnshire Road Car 1937 Leyland Tiger TS7 in spite of the Leyland Tiger Cub badge.

My first sighting of a low-floor bus, a Neoplan in the Dutch city The Hague, in 1988. Could such vehicles catch on in the UK?

with the tramway in the city centre, and when I visited in 2011 it was operated by 20 Mercedes-Benz Citaro G bendybuses. It quickly became a victim of its own success with buses that were so crowded at the peaks that a 3min frequency was introduced. Again, the plan was to convert it to a tramway when passenger figures reached the appropriate levels.

The daddy of all the busways was the Essen scheme in Germany, introduced in 1980. This was a guided busway and much of it ran between carriageways of a busy urban motorway. On my 1993 visit the busway was served by diesel bendybuses as well as trolleybuses with their booms down, running on batteries.

Brits abroad

UK-built buses were hard to find on mainland Europe until relatively recently, where Alexander Dennis, Optare and Wrightbus have enjoyed some export success. Many years before this there were pockets of British-built buses in northern Europe – in Denmark, the Netherlands and Sweden – and in southern Europe in Spain and, in greater numbers, Portugal.

Copenhagen took tri-axle Volvo B7Ls in 2001 with East Lancs bodies built in Blackburn, which were later pensioned off without their roofs as tourist sightseeing buses. Before that, Stockholm bought Park Royal-bodied Leyland Atlanteans and Panthers when the Swedish rule of the road

changed to right-hand running in 1967. There had been British-built double-deckers in Spain, and more recently there were these Dennis Darts.

Less obviously British-built were the buses in Malta in 2003. At the City Gate Square terminus just outside Valletta's city walls you could find a bewildering variety of elderly but amazing-looking yellow and orange buses proclaiming themselves to be things they quite obviously were not. But what were they?

It was difficult to find out. Engine sounds were sometimes a clue, but there were buses sporting chrome Leyland Tiger Cub badges that were clearly no such thing, and former London AEC Swifts declaring themselves to be AEC Reliances. Maltese engineers were clearly experienced at prolonging the lives of their buses, and their signwriters went to town with added decoration, inside and out.

The Maltese buses merely displayed very large route numbers – no destination information – which sometimes made for exciting journeys into the unknown. I later discovered that one of the 'Tiger Cubs' I photographed was actually a 1937 ex-Lincolnshire Road Car Leyland Tiger, and a chrome-bedecked confection had started out life as a 1938 Midland General AEC Regal. We may never know how much of the originals survived, if any, but in 2003 these classic types were living on borrowed time as newer secondhand buses were imported to be joined by brand new low-floor buses.

Closer to home, and the destination for my first proper trip – much more exciting than that day trip to Calais – was to Amsterdam in the early 1970s where I was pleased to see yellow buses proclaiming they were Leylands – and in this case they really were – as well as catching my first glimpse of bendybuses, Mercedes-Benz in the city fleet.

On a later trip to it was equally exciting to find my first low-floor bus, a Neoplan in the HTM fleet in The Hague. At the time I am sure I doubted that such continental fripperies as bendybuses and low floors would ever catch on in the UK. Not for the first time, I was wrong.

And Portugal? Well – on many, many visits to Portugal since the mid-1980s I have witnessed the number of British-built buses reduce from hundreds spread throughout the country to just a handful of preserved examples. AEC had the greatest success, supplying single-deck and double-deck models to a variety of fleets, followed by Leyland and Daimler, again with single- and double-deckers, as well as a few Guys, some masquerading as Daimlers.

Glimpses of individuality

With the growth of pan-European models, it was probably inevitable that the buses you can find today in most mainland European countries are similar to many of those on UK streets. It makes sense for a manufacturer to offer a limited range of buses, often complete buses rather than just chassis, but it is always a pleasure to discover buses on familiar chassis with locally-built bodies.

The Lisbon city operator, Carris, bought British-built chassis for many years. This is a 1967 three-doored UTIC-bodied Guy Victory CVU6LX badged as a Daimler, as Carris bought Fleetline double-deckers the same year. It was still in service in 1987.

Some of these stick fairly closely to the looks of the manufacturer's own body styling, while others trumpet their individuality. And as more bus builders emerge from around the world offering electric and now hydrogen buses, it seems likely that more of the individuality will disappear.

But in between the fleets of near-identical MAN, Mercedes-Benz, Scania and Volvo products, there are still glimpses of that individuality which can range from the attractive to the downright weird. Enjoy them while you can, for that is surely part of the fun of travelling beyond our shores, travelling hopefully with no real preconceptions, prepared to be impressed, amused or disappointed.

If abroad starts at Calais, there is no reason why it should stop there. ■

The Portuguese city of Porto bought 15 Berlin-style MAN Lion's City double-deckers in 2011; previous double-deck generations there were Leyland Atlanteans and Lancia trolleybuses in the 1960s.

Cleveland Transit 955 (OIB 3512), originally registered D455 GHN, was one of the last Royal Tiger Doyens built. It was new to the Teesside municipal company in July 1987 and was sold to Delta of Stockton-on-Tees in July 1995. Geoff Mills photographed it in Windsor in May 1992.

Royal Tiger Doyen

Leyland's rear-engined integral coach of the 1980s is the subject of this photograph selection taken by GEOFF MILLS

The Royal Tiger Doyen was Leyland's answer to the influx of imported rear-engined coaches in the 1980s, a premium integral construction model launched in November 1982 to complement the mid-engined Tiger. It had either the Leyland TL11 or Cummins L10 engine.

Production began at Leyland's Charles H Roe factory in Leeds which closed in 1984, after which it was built at the Lillyhall plant near Workington that opened in 1971 to manufacture the Leyland National. The Doyen name was appended to the complete vehicle, as Leyland also offered the Royal Tiger underframe to third party bodybuilders.

Sales did not reach expectations and this was one of the first models that Volvo dropped after acquiring Leyland Bus in 1988. Bus Lists on the Web shows that, apart from prototypes, just 99 Royal Tiger Doyens were built, 42 by Roe and 57 at Lillyhall. There were 65 other Royal Tiger underframes, 37 bodied by Plaxton and 28 by Van Hool. National Bus Company subsidiaries took 43 Doyens, the Scottish Bus Group six. ∎

C441 HHL was the last coach bought new by Charles Cook of Biggleswade, in October 1985, using it for the company's long established continental holiday programme. It remained in the fleet until April 1996 and moved on to Elite of Stockport for just over two years, after which it passed to a Merseyside operator as a source of spare parts. It was visiting Bury St Edmunds in August 1994. Cook also operated a secondhand Royal Tiger with Van Hool Alizée body.

This Doyen was registered D160 HML when new to Jacobs of Fair Oak, Hampshire in May 1987. It had become 3150 RU when visiting Weymouth in September 1994, shortly before it was sold for further service in various English fleets.

This was the first Royal Tiger Doyen built at Lillyhall after production transferred from Roe at Leeds. It was first registered A483 MHG in May 1984 as a Leyland demonstrator and had become DXI 1454 when Shropshire operator Butters of Childs Ercall took it to Wembley in March 1995. It had four operator owners before Butters bought it in September 1992.

The **Tens** and the **Sevens**

JOHN DEEGAN recalls two batches of Ulsterbus Bristol REs operated in Derry~Londonderry, one bought new, the other secondhand and how most succumbed to rioters and hijackers

Alexander-bodied Bristol RELL6L 1054 (9054 UZ) was chosen for the official photographs, taken by company employee and Buses Irish Journey contributor Reg Ludgate. When new, they wore the half Riviera Blue, half Trader Ivory livery, but later received the brighter livery. ULSTERBUS/PAUL SAVAGE COLLECTION

Over 50 years have passed since Ulsterbus placed its first 20 Bristol REs in service. That was 1969, and those Leyland-engined RELLs were followed by over 600 similar but Gardner-engined Bristols, which gained a cult reputation with enthusiasts.

After the trial of ECW-bodied demonstrator LAE 770E in 1967, Ulsterbus ordered the 20 RELL6Ls, which were bodied by Alexander in Falkirk to Potter design with 44 seats and two doors. They were numbered 1051-70 (9051-70 UZ) and entered service in Derry early in 1969, the year that the Troubles began. Subsequent events accounted for the loss of 19 of the 20.

When new, they were allocated to the main city service routes and in particular the cross-city Altnagelvin-Rosemount run, but they would be particularly associated later on with the Creggan route (C). They were delivered in a distinctive livery with the lower panels painted all blue, but later received the updated less blue, more ivory scheme.

Street disturbances in Ulster became a way of life and a regular occurrence in Derry. The first RE taken in a riot was 1055, at Rosemount in August 1969. It was then used, for several days, as a barricade before being swapped for a redundant Leyland Tiger PS1 after local management struck a deal with the people who had seized it. That PS1 was towed to the site by a company Land Rover, but when the hijackers discovered the PS1 was shorter than the RE, they took the Land Rover as well, to fill the gap.

Such a deal would not be repeated as the riots became more frequent. Indeed, the newest members of this batch had very short lives. The first to be destroyed was 1069, in July 1971 when barely two years old. Next to go was 1053 in September 1972; it had attended the 1971 Irish Transport Trust rally and was lost in Creggan, as were most that met a premature end.

Three more were hijacked in 1973. The last of the batch, 1070, was destroyed in Creggan during May, while 1060 was taken at Shantallow estate in July and 1063 was seized in Creggan. My interest in buses began around this time when I witnessed two REs being driven past my house in Creggan by a group of around 20 youths. I know at least one of the REs was burned at the Creggan terminus that night; it may well have been 1063.

Things went a bit quieter the following year as only one Bristol was destroyed, 1068 taken in Shantallow in October 1974.

New Bristols arrive

The next part of the RE story began in 1975, as 2001-28 (JOI 3001-28), the first of the Gardner 6HLX-engined RELL6Gs, hit Derry's streets. Besides their engines, these differed from the 1969 Bristols in having twin headlights, a more modern front grille and forced air ventilation in place of opening vents.

For many years, these buses were kept well away from the Creggan and Lone Moor routes which were the most risky for hijackings, so the remaining 1969 Bristols were left to the mercies of the Creggan route along with the remaining AEC

Reliances. Besides the estate itself, the Creggan route also takes in William Street in the Bogside, another hijacking hotspot, hence Ulsterbus wanting its newer vehicles on other city routes.

Only one more 1969 bus was lost between 1975 and 1977. That was 1065, hijacked and burned at Central Drive, Creggan on July 27, 1976 after a night of severe rioting. But a quarter of the original 20 were destroyed in 1978, 1056/7/61/4 in one go, when Pennyburn depot was bombed in February, followed in August when 1054 was seized.

The annual Apprentice Boys parade around August 12 usually ended up with violence erupting in the Bogside and two years on the trot, 1979 and 1980, the Falkirk Bristols were caught up in the aftermath, with 1062 seized in William Street in 1979, barely minutes into its trip to Creggan.

The following year, the week of the parade saw three losses. On August 9, 1059 was seized around 07:00 at Westland Street by a group who then abandoned it before it crashed into a house halfway down the street; luckily there were no casualties. It spent the next two years in Limavady depot yielding parts. Then 1052 was destroyed at William Street on August 12; ITN News coverage of this is on You Tube. Two days later I witnessed 1055 being destroyed at the Creggan terminus. The area manager told the *Derry Journal* he had lost half his Creggan fleet in that week alone.

ECW-bodied Bristol RELL6L demonstrator LAE 770E on trial in November 1967 on the Shantallow-Clooney route. It was a two-door 35-seater. HOWARD CUNNINGHAM

Leyland-engined Bristols returned to Derry in April 1986 when five ECW-bodied RESL6Ls from Ribble were drafted in to help cover losses. This was 719 (OCK 346K) turning into Water Street in the city centre. It survived for about 18 months before being destroyed in the Bogside in November 1987.

That left just 1051/8/66/7, two of which stood out from the rest. After front end damage around 1978, 1066 gained a new front with twin headlights, like the RELL6Gs with Alexander (Belfast) bodies built at Mallusk, while 1067 had rear end treatment and gained the nearside 'elephant's ear' air intake found on the newer Bristols.

Kept off the Creggan run

There were many days of unrest in 1981 when Republican prisoners staged their fatal hunger strike, and as a precaution the remaining Falkirk-built REs spent much of that year away from the Creggan route. When the route did run, ex-Ribble and Southdown Leyland Leopards were provided.

Moving the remaining 'Tens' on to safer routes did not prevent two losses in 1981. In May, 1067 was seized in Rosemount and taken to Creggan and crashed. Although a bit like the 1059 hijacking mentioned earlier, 1067 was not as badly damaged but still written off. In a rather daring hijack, 1066 was taken in Spencer Road in the Waterside, driven across the Craigavon Bridge to the Bogside and burned.

The two survivors, 1051 and 1058, spent much of 1982 away from the Creggan route, as there was again much unrest on Derry's streets; 1051 became the regular Rosemount bus for a while.

Their association with the Creggan route ended in 1983. On March 16, 1051 was on its usual late

Creggan duty and the 21:50 journey that night was very quiet. I was the only passenger, with driver Johnny McLaughlin, when one stop before the terminus two men boarded, produced a large knife and ordered us off. Half an hour later, 1051 was gone. Two nights later the same driver was hijacked, in the same area, with 1058. It was doused in petrol but recovered by the army, undamaged.

It was hijacked again in July, in William Street, taken to the Rossville Flats and badly damaged, although this cat with nine lives lived to see another day as the garage staff in Derry spent many months rebuilding it, though it did end up with a dashboard for a Mallusk-built RE. Such was the time and expense in repairing 1058 that when it went back into service, it was decided that its Creggan days were over.

It was employed on the early Curryneirin duty and an afternoon stint on the Nelson Drive route, although it did show up on other routes as well. When withdrawn in 1985, 1058 passed into preservation.

The secondhand REs

By the early 1980s, the Derry City fleet as a whole had taken a real battering with the continuing street violence. Various Leopards, including the ex-Ribble and Southdown examples, provided the riskier city routes like Creggan, Lone Moor and Shantallow. Bristol LHs were drafted in as well, but none of them were really suitable for city work, the

Leopards because of their high entrance steps and the LHs with their manual gears.

Citybus in Belfast had been receiving ex-National Bus Company (NBC) ECW-bodied REs for several years, and in June 1983 some were diverted to Ulsterbus for Derry City services. The first to arrive were ex-West Yorkshire Road Car RELL6Gs numbered 752-6 (MWW 753/4K, VWT 683L, TWX 197L, LWU 543K) and shorter RESL6Gs 765–7 (OWY 749/51/2K); 767 entered service with interior advertisements for West Yorkshire PTE tickets. All except 765 met with fiery ends, though it also was hijacked and lost all its windows; it was then used for spares.

Next to arrive, from United Auto in early 1985, were RELLs 782/3 (OHN 459/60L) and RESLs 786/7 (GHN 445/6J). The drivers at Pennyburn disliked them as both mechanically and body wise they were in poor condition compared to the West Yorkshire examples; United had fitted 782 and 786 with grilles for the Bristol LH.

Four more RELL6Gs arrived in the Maiden City later that year, this time from Eastern National. They were 788/9/95/6 (LVX 116J, MHK 914J, WNO 539/40L) and were good performers, 788/9 being quite nippy; 795 became the dedicated Creggan bus. By the time these entered service, several ex-NBC REs had been lost, with 753 only lasting around a month on the Creggan service before it was seized, and 752/4/6/66/7/87 also were destroyed.

Derry was again using Leopards, elderly Potter-bodied examples included, until more REs could be sourced.

The sound of the Leyland-engined RE made a welcome return to the city in 1986 with the arrival of RESL6Ls 719-23 (OCK 346/51K, NCK 331/5/4J) from Ribble with seats in that company's attractive red moquette. These were lively performers, many of the 'old school' drivers saying they were just like the 'Tens' when tackling the hill up to Creggan, although the bodywork of 722 and 723 was in poor shape.

During its first week in service, 723 still had its Ribble destination blind and was noted doing a late Slievemore showing Blackpool as its destination; 722 became the regular Rosemount bus after the loss of loaned Citybus allover advertising RELL6G 2560 (AXI 2560). These were the last ECW-bodied REs sent to Derry, as newer Alexander-bodied Bristols were coming from other depots.

The ECW era was coming to an end in 1988 when I witnessed an example of indomitable human spirit. I was a passenger on 795 when four youths seized it at Central Drive, Creggan, and while helping a rather feisty old lady off the bus with her shopping trolley, she gave the four hijackers a right good verbal and nearly clattered one of them with her brolly, even though the rear of 795 was already on fire.

With the arrival of ten new 48-seat Leyland Tigers at the end of 1988, surviving ECW-bodied Bristols 721/2/3/89 were transferred to Citybus for limited use on schools and driving schools duties; 723 was only used for spares recovery.

Thus ended an era that, although being tough times in which to operate bus services, provided enthusiasts with much variety.

Sole survivor of the 'Tens' is 1058 (9058 UZ). After being hijacked and fire-damaged in July 1983, it was rebuilt and served until 1985 when it was sold for preservation. PAUL SAVAGE

Bristol REs in Northern Ireland

Northern Ireland's association with the Bristol RE began in February 1966, when Belfast Corporation Transport trialled West Yorkshire Road Car SRG15 (HWU 641C), an ECW-bodied Bristol RELL6G new in 1965, as part of its search for suitable one-man-operated single-deckers.

It also borrowed AEC Swift, Daimler Roadliner and Leyland Panther demonstrators and inspected a Leyland Panther Cub lent by Manchester Corporation, before ordering Swifts and Roadliners. The Ulster Transport Authority, soon to transfer its buses to Ulsterbus, also inspected the RE and the three demonstrators.

ECW-bodied RELL6L demonstrator LAE 770E reached Ulsterbus's Duncrue Street works in Belfast on October 30, 1967, was sent to Derry~Londonderry two days later for trials on the cross-city Rosemount-Altnagelvin and Shantallow-Clooney routes where it was compared with the Swift demonstrator.

This led Ulsterbus to order the 20 RELL6Ls in 1967; they were delivered between December 1968 and early January 1969, replacing 42-seat AEC Reliances on Derry City routes. Ulsterbus had asked Bristol to quote for REs with the AEC AH691 engine, which would have made them RELL6A, a type never built.

The next 40 were ordered for delivery in 1975, RELL6Gs with Gardner engine and bodies built at Alexander's Mallusk factory. Of these, 2001-28 (JOI 3001-28) were dual-door 44-seaters for Derry and Craigavon, while 50-seat single-door 2029-40 (JOI 3029-40) went to Bangor and Oxford Street, Belfast.

Leyland kept the Bristol RE in production for Ulsterbus and Citybus, as well as some export markets. Ulsterbus bought a further 220 until the model ceased to be available in 1983. Citybus received 340, both dual-door and single-door, with various seating layouts, placing them in service between 1976 and 1986.

As John Deegan relates, the Troubles took a toll on buses. Some REs lasted only days before being destroyed. Among 19 buses destroyed when the IRA attacked Pennyburn depot on February 19, 1978, Bristols 2206/7/9 (POI 2206/7/9) had only been delivered in preceding days and may never have turned a wheel in service.

By the mid-1970s, the level of destruction was becoming unsustainable and after acquiring secondhand single-deck Daimler Fleetlines for Citybus, attention turned to London Transport for AEC Merlins. Ulsterbus received 22 in 1977, but they were not the most suitable vehicles.

National Bus Company subsidiaries were by then withdrawing REs and 176 were sourced, most for use in Belfast with Citybus, but 21 from West Yorkshire Road Car, United, Eastern National and Ribble went to Derry between 1983 and 1986.

As new vehicles arrived and the situation improved, Citybus and Ulsterbus sold on redundant RELL6Gs, with 46 passing between 1991 and 1993 to Bus Éireann as schoolbuses, and 33 (including five for spares recovery) went to the Londonderry & Lough Swilly Railway Company between 2003 and 2005.

The RE era ended in 2004, the last with Citybus going on Saturday January 31. Those at Ulsterbus were scheduled to finish after a five-vehicle tour at Derry on Saturday February 28, but as that was a leap year, 2595 (BXI 2595) went out on a late Sunday duty until almost midnight.

Even that was not the end. Their replacement vehicles had not arrived, so 2570/95/6/8 were relicensed on the Monday and served for another month while 2440 (WOI 2440) survived at Coleraine until May. Four of Lough Swilly's worked until October 2007 and another until November. ∎

By PAUL SAVAGE

West Yorkshire SRG15 on trial with Belfast Corporation in February 1966. BELFAST TELEGRAPH

There are at least three Alexander-bodied Bristol RELL6Gs in this scene in Derry. Citybus 2560 (AXI 2560), with allover advertisement for coal, was on loan to Ulsterbus, with paper bill in the windscreen indicating that it was the regular bus on the Rosemount service at the time. It was hijacked and destroyed in August 1989. The 'elephant's ear' nearside rear air intake is apparent on it and the bus in front. PAUL SAVAGE

Bus Éireann BG36 (77 D 213), photographed at Longford in August 1994, was one of 46 RELL6Gs acquired from Northern Ireland. It was originally Ulsterbus 2192 (POI 2192). PAUL SAVAGE

Cheshire in the 2020s

MP Travel, based in Higher Walton, Warrington, operated the X1 service between Runcorn and Liverpool on behalf of Arriva until it was withdrawn on April 2, 2022. Two Alexander Dennis Enviro200 MMCs entered service in May 2021 in heritage liveries of two companies that ran on the Runcorn Busway to celebrate its 50 years of operation. Leaving Runcorn High Street bus station on its first day in service, May 19, 2021, is EX21 ONE in Crosville Busway livery with orange stripe; similar TX21 ONE wore North Western's red, blue and yellow Busway livery.

JOHN ROBINSON takes a photographic bus tour around the county of Cheshire to show some of the variety of operators providing services today

The county of Cheshire took its current form on April 1, 1974 when much of the Wirral peninsula, including Birkenhead and Wallasey, passed into the newly-formed metropolitan county of Merseyside and similarly, in north-east Cheshire, towns including Stockport and Stalybridge passed into the new metropolitan county of Greater Manchester.

These metropolitan counties bounded one another in the area between St Helens and Wigan, both hitherto in Lancashire, effectively cutting off the south of the Red Rose county, with the result that Warrington and Widnes, previously in Lancashire, found themselves in Cheshire. While the boundaries have not changed since then, Cheshire is now made up of four unitary authorities: Cheshire West & Chester, Cheshire East, Halton and Warrington.

Just before bus services were deregulated in October 1986, Crosville was by far the biggest operator in Cheshire in terms of number of routes operated. Relatively minor, by comparison, incursions into the county were made by other National Bus Company subsidiaries East Midland, Potteries, Ribble and Trent.

The county also boasted three municipal operators: Chester City Transport, Halton Transport and Warrington Borough Transport, Greater Manchester Transport and Merseyside Transport provided PTE representation while a handful of independents provided services within or into Cheshire.

The 2020s picture is much changed and the only tangible link with these pre-deregulation times is Warrington Borough Transport, which currently trades as Warrington's Own Buses and, at the time of writing, was one of only eight arm's length municipal operators left in Great Britain.

The major operator in Cheshire now is Arriva, which has taken over much of the former Crosville territory in the county, together with some routes originating in such neighbouring parts of Wales as Flint, Mold and Wrexham into Cheshire. Other operators with a significant presence are Stagecoach and Centrebus-owned D&G Bus.

This feature shows a cross-section of the operators, as well the diverse landscape of the county. The pictures are broadly set out to represent a journey starting in Runcorn, crossing the Silver Jubilee Bridge to Widnes and from there following a clockwise circular route via Chester to Parkgate. ■

Arguably the most iconic engineering structure in Cheshire is the Grade II listed Silver Jubilee Bridge across the River Mersey and Manchester Ship Canal at Runcorn Gap, linking the towns of Widnes and Runcorn. Opened in 1961 to replace an adjacent transporter bridge, its carriageway was widened between 1975 and 1977, after which the bridge was given its official name in honour of the Queen's Silver Jubilee. Crossing on April 2, 2022, operating service 62 from Halebank, Widnes to Murdishaw, Runcorn, is Arriva North West 5015 (OW17 WNG), a Caetano-bodied MAN 18.270 EcoCity, one of 19 of these gas-fuelled buses in the fleet, all based at the former Crosville depot in Runcorn.

The collapse of council-owned Halton Transport in January 2020 resulted in many services passing to Ashcroft's, Arriva North West and Warrington's Own Buses. Operating service 27A from Barrows Green, Ashcroft's Alexander Dennis Pointer Dart HIG 8904 approaches the terminus at West Bank, Widnes on March 8, 2022. It was new to Stagecoach South in 2004.

HTL Buses (Huyton Travel Ltd), has a fleet of around 40 vehicles on services in Merseyside, over half of them Optare Solos. Typifying these is YJ11 EKP, one of eight new in May 2011, operating service 39 from St Helens to Wargrave. Although both these towns are in Merseyside, the route runs for a short distance through Cheshire where it is seen in Chapel Lane, Burtonwood on March 8, 2022.

Warrington's Own Buses Volvo B7TL/Alexander ALX 400 153 (V141 LGC) at the Harrison Square, Dallam terminus on March 17, 2022 before leaving for the Bus Interchange on service 16A. New as Go-Ahead London Central AVL41 in February 2000, it was the final survivor of a batch acquired by Warrington in 2011, its first low-floor double-deckers. This is one of two double-deckers in the fleet wearing this attractive livery for Warrington & Vale Royal College, the other being Wright Pulsar Gemini-bodied DAF DB250 186.

Go North West began operations in June 2019 following the Go-Ahead Group's purchase of First Manchester's Queens Road depot with around 160 vehicles. Its only service into Cheshire is the 100 from Manchester Shudehill to Warrington, historically the jointly-operated Salford City Transport and Lancashire United Transport service 10. On March 31, 2022 MCV EvoSeti-bodied Volvo B5LH 3070 (BV66 VKZ), numerically the last of 20 transferred from Go-Ahead London, which were converted to single-doorway before entering service in Manchester, pulls away from its stop at the Black Swan in Hollins Green, just over the border from Greater Manchester.

Centrebus-owned D&G Bus operates many services in Cheshire. Wright StreetLite WF (wheel-forward) 155 (MX11 EGE) stands in Knutsford bus station on April 3, 2021, operating service 88 from Altrincham to Macclesfield. This bus came to D&G in December 2014 when the services of Biddulph, Staffordshire-based BakerBus were purchased with nine buses, although it was new to Speke, Liverpool-based Supertravel.

D&G did not operate service 88 on Sundays, when Go-Goodwins' Little Gem provided a curtailed service between Wilmslow and Altrincham where, at the time, it operated a network of local services. New contracts starting on 24 April, 2022 saw most of these lost to Arriva and Sunday operation of the 88 ceased. Just before these changes, on March 13, 2022, Optare Metrocity 1945 (GSU 489) was heading along Water Lane, Wilmslow towards the terminus in Bank Square. It was new as YJ15 AAU to APH in July 2015 for operations at Gatwick Airport.

The only First route in Cheshire is the half-hourly service 3 between Hanley and Crewe operated by First Potteries. The Potteries branding adorns Wright StreetLite Max 63173 (SN64 CGG), new in September 2014, which was heading back to Hanley as picked up at Bank Corner, Alsager on May 16, 2022.

High Peak Buses was formed in April 2012 as a joint venture between Centrebus, which in June 2007 had acquired the business of Eric W Bowers of Chapel-en-le-Frith), and Wellglade Group's Trent Barton depot at Dove Holes. It operates around 40 buses, including Optare Solo SR 283 (YD63 VFJ) photographed as it approached Macclesfield along the A537 Buxton New Road near Walker Barn on March 27, 2022 on a service 58 journey from Buxton to Macclesfield.

Nantwich Aqueduct, constructed around 1826, with Thomas Telford as consulting engineer, carries the main line of the Shropshire Union Canal over the Chester to Nantwich road and is Grade II* listed. Passing the impressive structure on April 18, 2022, operating service 84 from Chester to Crewe, is Arriva North West 2934 (MX09 EKO), a Wright Pulsar 2-bodied VDL SB200 new to Arriva Manchester in April 2009.

Aintree Coachline operates service 41 between Chester railway station and Whitchurch in neighbouring Shropshire. Operating the 13:20 service from Whitchurch on May 5, 2022, Alexander Dennis Enviro200 121 (YX65 RFN), new in October 2015, was passing through the village of Tattenhall. It is branded for Chester's City Rail Link service 40 which utilises the former Chester City Transport colours of maroon and cream.

Chester has three park-&-ride routes operated by Stagecoach, which took over First's business in the city in 2012 including the former Chester City Transport operations. Alexander Dennis Enviro200 MMC 26053 (SN16 OPH) was turning into Chester Bus Interchange on March 6, 2022 while operating the PR2 to Boughton Heath. This Chester West & Chester Council livery was superseded during 2022 by a pale blue-based scheme.

Arrowebrook Coaches, operating from the village of Croughton, roughly midway between Chester and Ellesmere Port, ran service 26 between Ellesmere Port and Guilden Sutton via Chester. After completing the final service of the day on 5 April, 2022, the 15:32 short working from Guilden Sutton to Wervin, TransBus Super Pointer Dart SN53 AVG was negotiating the hump-backed bridge over the Shropshire Union Canal in Wervin Road, Croughton as it approached the depot. It was new in October 2003 to Lothian (as its 93) and saw subsequent service with Ipswich (numbered 134), whose livery it still carried.

Parkgate is a village on the Wirral peninsula on the banks of the River Dee, adjoining 100sqkm of salt marsh. Before the Dee silted up to form the marsh, Parkgate was a thriving port and seaside resort but as the silting progressed it lost its beach and direct access to the sea. Heading along The Parade on 17 May, 2022, Al's of Birkenhead Alexander Dennis Enviro200 MMC CC21 ALS was passing between The Middle Slip, where the Parkgate fishermen used to land their catches at high tide, and The Old Watch House, once used by the coastguard and, later, HM Customs before becoming a private house. It was operating service 22 from West Kirby to Chester, which was historically Crosville's service C22.

South Yorks cover shots

From 1983 to 1986, **MIKE GREENWOOD** took the photographs for the covers of South Yorkshire PTE's timetable books. These tell the evolving story of what then was a radically different and controversial approach to public transport provision.

I joined South Yorkshire Passenger Transport Executive's operations and marketing department as information officer in July 1983. The main purpose of my job, as per my job description, was 'to present in understandable and acceptable manner information with regard to all passenger transport services and facilities within the South Yorkshire County; to ensure that such information was distributed and maintained by the operating districts and/or other companies concerned'.

In reality this translated into organising publicity and promotional material, working with outside designers and consultancies to promote new services and facilities such as services for the disabled plus new fare-related initiatives such as weekly tickets and Savercard.

I had started my transport career, in 1972, with my home town operator of Leicester City Transport and had received a good grounding in all the different facets of traffic operation including a two year period as traffic trainee and had also been put through the driving school and obtained my PSV licence.

By October 1982 I had risen to the position of traffic officer (planning and publicity), a date

One of the PTE's newly delivered Mk2 MCW Metrobuses in Sheffield in 1983.

Sheffield and Rotherham
Bus/Rail Times

6th November 1983 until further notice

Alexander-bodied Dennis Dominator 2101 in 1984 in the Bus & Coach Council's 'We'd all miss the bus' campaign which had been launched two years earlier.

Northern Counties-bodied Dominator 2312, new the previous year and passing Sheffield station, in 1984. Gracing the back cover was preserved Sheffield Corporation 904, a Roe-bodied Leyland Titan PD3/1 built in 1959.

Alexander-bodied Dominator 2269 at Rotherham for a 1985 book. By then, the political fight against deregulation put a Park Royal-bodied Daimler Fleetline campaign bus on the back cover.

which coincided with the withdrawal of the final Leyland Titan PD3s. Leicester City Transport was a well-respected, efficient and forward looking municipal operator but South Yorkshire PTE was at a far higher level.

Pro-public transport

Formed in April 1974 in an area where car ownership per head was lower than the national average, the PTE was early in recognising the opportunity for reducing traffic congestion by

Transport integration is emphasised in 1985 by an Alexander-bodied Leyland Atlantean at Chapeltown station as a British Rail Metro-Cammell diesel multiple unit stands overhead. The back cover uses a Plaxton Paramount-bodied Dennis Dorchester to promote coach hire.

A Yorkshire Traction Series B Leyland National 2 in special service livery in 1985.

encouraging the use of public transport, and the necessary steps were taken and plans put into place.

A concerted programme of platform staff recruitment and vehicle upgrading and replacement resulted in passenger carrying figures steadily increasing. This was against the national trend and South Yorkshire was unique among the seven PTEs in achieving this. There was also a low-fare policy and heavy financial subsidy from South Yorkshire Metropolitan County Council which caused controversy in some places but definitely resulted in significant modal shift.

It was certainly an interesting and exciting time to be working for South Yorkshire PTE when I joined because the grand design, initiated in 1974, was fully coming to fruition in the early 1980s.

Early on, the PTE combined the services in the former Sheffield and Rotherham municipal areas into a single timetable book with a print run of about 25,000 copies. It was, in the main, published twice a year. The first Sheffield & Rotherham book, published in May 1974, was 6½in by 4in in size and had 368 pages.

The first timetable book for which I provided a cover photograph was issue number 17 with a cover date of November 1983. This had 428 pages, reflecting the expansion of service provision over the years. By this time, the print run had also grown to 27,000 copies per edition.

The size and nature of the books fell into the category of a small format paperback which meant that print tender invitations attracted responses from the large firms who printed paperback books using modern automated printing and binding machines. They could meet the PTE's requirement for a fast turnaround but it did impose new disciplines on the PTE staff in the operations and marketing section who were responsible for publicity.

Slots for machine time had to be reserved some time ahead and could not be varied. If the copy was not ready and the slot was missed it might be

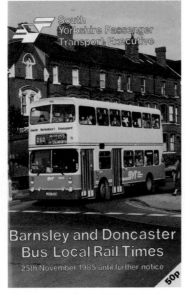

The then new South Yorkshire's Transport livery on an Alexander-bodied Atlantean in Doncaster while a back cover view of a Yorkshire Traction Bristol LHS with The Nipper branding represents Barnsley.

several months before it could be rescheduled. The PTE would be sharing machine time with publishers of new fiction paperbacks which had firm dates for launching and publication.

Printing on this scale used the web-offset process, meaning the machines printed reels of paper on the web, instead of on to the sheets of paper used by more traditional printing processes, thus ensuring a faster print time. We were told that 25,000 books could be printed in 30 to 45min. Covers were printed separately, often weeks in advance as they were in full colour and printed on card.

Barnsley & Doncaster

The Barnsley & Doncaster combined area PTE timetable book came along sometime later, as in 1974 Yorkshire Traction was still publishing its own timetables which gave coverage of services in

The final pre-deregulation book for Sheffield & Rotherham had a Dominator on the front and a new Leyland-DAB bendybus on the back.

Mike Greenwood's equivalent book for Barnsley & Doncaster had a Yorkshire Traction Leyland Olympian meeting a PTE Dominator on the level crossing at Barnsley station. The back cover showed one of the PTE's Alexander-bodied Leyland Leopards converted to accommodate wheelchair users.

Barnsley. The PTE published one Doncaster District timetable book, dated April 1975.

The first combined PTE timetable book for Barnsley & Doncaster was published in October 1976. The format for this was the same as for the Sheffield & Rotherham book and it had 332 pages.

Demand for timetables was never as great in Barnsley and Doncaster, so print runs of 6,000 to 7,000 copies were all that were needed and the books were published just once a year. Smaller printing firms could be used and they could be printed from sheets instead of from the web, as this book contained fewer pages than the Sheffield & Rotherham book, but sometimes the larger firms were successful in winning the contract.

The first Barnsley & Doncaster book for which I supplied a cover photo was the 404-page edition number 8, dated July 1984.

Photographs appeared on the front and back covers of the timetable books and I endeavoured to get in-service shots for the front covers including the combination of bus and rail services on a few occasions. The opportunity to capture newly delivered vehicles, new liveries or new service initiatives was also part of the thinking in creating a suitable composition.

The back covers, however, were often more of a promotional nature including attempts to increase the awareness of the private hire fleet, so we sometimes used posed shots I had taken.

Thwarted by big changes

The continuation of South Yorkshire PTE's low-fare policy was thwarted by a combination of the Transport Act 1985 which deregulated bus services and required PTEs to set up arm's length operating companies and by the abolition of South Yorkshire and the other metropolitan councils on March 31, 1986.

My involvement with SYPTE timetables and providing colour photographs stopped with deregulation, although the books continued to be published until March 1989. However, there no longer were photographs on the covers.

The last two area SYPTE timetable books for which I supplied photographs were the 552-page Sheffield & Rotherham number 22, which was valid from May 19, 1986 until October 25, 1986 (the last day of regulated bus services) and had 552 pages, and the 384-page Barnsley & Doncaster number 11, valid from July 19, 1986 also until October 25.

At deregulation I transferred to the new arm's length South Yorkshire Transport company, the one that later renamed itself Mainline, as customer services manager and faced a multitude of new challenges.

I would like to acknowledge the invaluable assistance of my friend and former SYPTE colleague John Hardey in providing a massive amount of helpful information. ∎

The first of United Counties` second-hand invasion was 948 (LFW 320), a 1955 Bristol Lodekka LD6B bought from Lincolnshire Road Car in 1971. Fitted with a five-speed gearbox, it made itself useful on Bedford`s longer routes, including the epic 128 from Northampton to Cambridge. It was nearly at the end of its days here, setting off from Northampton`s Derngate bus station on the 50mile hike, still sporting its original long apron front.

Secondhand woes

Most of us have a favourite decade and for **LAURENCE KNIGHT** it was the 1970s, even if it was not for his local National Bus Company operator, United Counties

It could have been written for me. "I don`t like Mondays," wailed the Boom Town Rats, and in 1971 Mondays were doubly cursed to this then 12-year-old. School was a bad enough ordeal – I could never understand after my first day there why I had to go back – but Monday night was dreaded Boys` Brigade night, generally spent scrambling around a splintery church room playing "crab football". As if football of the "proper" variety was not enough of a waste of time, to my mind.

Instead of subjecting myself to removing splinters from my hand throughout the coming week, it was an easy decision to remain on the United Counties Bristol KSW that took me to town. I spent my 6d

(2½p) "subs" on hot chocolate from the vending machine in Northampton's Derngate bus station, observing the fleet being washed and refuelled.

Next to the fuel pumps was the driver defect sheet, always good for a laugh; one truculent driver observed simply "Bus not fast enough". My beloved KSWs would be refuelled and lined up for the next morning`s runout, but occasionally one stayed out late.

A wet and windy winter`s night was one such occasion. I squeezed myself past three other passengers on a bench seat on the side-gangway upper deck of CNH 709, and our departure was heralded by the usual Bristol second gear sounds — a judder and a friendly chuckle. Cigarette smoke and condensation vied to obscure the dismal road ahead and droplets of nicotine-infused water plopped down my neck from the flat ceiling.

Such was travel as it used to be on United Counties buses, yet ten years later the oldest double-decker in the fleet would be a Bristol VR. Big changes were to take place on the bumpy journey that lay ahead.

Homework by candlelight

The 1970s was a difficult time for the bus industry, with widespread strikes compromising the delivery of both new buses and spare parts. Three-day weeks, riots, crew shortages and power cuts added to the gloom, and yet it was a fascinating time for the bus enthusiast. Secondhand purchases challenged the uniformity of many fleets, while faithful old halfcabs were retained or reinstated.

Maybe it was no coincidence that the high school I chose to attend happened to be just down the road from United Counties' Bedford Road central works. An extra incentive, not that one was needed, for me to be promptly away and on my bike at the 16:00 bell. Daily surprises lay in wait inside the entrance to the works, be it buses from "foreign" depots passing through for overhaul, accident victims, new deliveries or recent withdrawals.

But something was definitely afoot with the sighting of three ex-Lincolnshire Road Car Bristol Lodekka LD6Bs. All became clear a few weeks later when I found myself riding home on shiny, overhauled 917 (LFW 325), ominously taking the fleetnumber of a discarded KSW.

There had been a time when former Tilling Group companies only rarely acquired secondhand stock, but circumstances changed in the 1970s, certainly for the United Counties Omnibus Company, its usual buying policy being typically Tilling, typically conservative.

For many a year, its double-deckers — Bristol/ ECWs of course — could only have four-speed gearboxes and Bristol engines. The Lodekkas received in 1966 that were delivered as Gardner-engined FS6Gs owing to a wind-down in the supply of Bristol BVW engines caused apoplexy, and it was rumoured that they were nearly sent back.

By the early 1970s, however, United Counties was experiencing woes resulting from the purchase of the cash-strapped Luton Corporation's fleet, which had been neglected to the point of decrepitude in many cases. Renewing certificates of fitness was not an option for many of the non-standard Dennis

The problems that beset United Counties at the start of the 1970s were not helped by the many elderly Bristol KSW6Bs in need of replacement, like 870 (CNH 709) dating from 1952. These were mellow-sounding and great fun to ride on, but a journey in an upper deck of its lowbridge ECW body full of smokers on a cold winter`s night was a different proposition. Note the low ceiling and four-abreast seating. This 55-seater was a regular at Northampton, as was KS5G 838 (FRP 692) behind, now preserved by Graham Ledger. ROGER WARWICK

Passengers for Biggleswade have a choice of Bristol MW6Gs in Bedford bus station in 1974. Ex-Midland General 126 (26 DRB), new in 1958 and now with standard destination equipment, or 141 (TBD 141) new to United Counties a year later. Both still have coach seats. Lodekka FS6G 709 (HBD 709D) waits to leave for Hitchin.

Lolines and Albion Lowlanders inherited, since these had serious defects including cracked chassis.

They soon started to accumulate behind Bedford depot; a depressing sight, heavily cannibalised and standing on bricks in some cases. Forty-five double-deckers would need imminent replacement. Only the ex-Luton Bristol RE single-deckers were young enough, and standard enough, to see United Counties through the decade.

British Leyland was feeling the effects of the industrial unrest that characterised the decade. Not necessarily in its truck and bus plants, as cars were where the problems were at their worst, but this still affected the supply of new buses and spare parts, a situation compounded by Leyland's near-monopoly of the heavy-duty bus market.

This created problems for many operators, and the recertification of buses due for withdrawal was a common solution. West Midlands PTE stretched the lives of its antiquated ex-Birmingham Daimler CVG6s and Guy Arabs of 1950-54 without too much difficulty, and London Transport`s well-maintained RTs were afforded a wonderful Indian summer, popping up on Central Area routes scheduled for Routemasters. DMS-class Fleetlines, meanwhile, languished in depots awaiting spares.

The fact that several operators extended the lives of their oldest buses during the 1970s was undoubtedly down to the new bus famine, but also was an indication that some halfcabs were being scrapped before their time in the rush to convert to one-person operation.

Battling on several fronts

For United Counties, there were further problems. Most of its double-deckers built between 1951 and 1958 were Bristol AVW-powered – a wonderfully mellow and smooth-running engine — but spares for these engines were out of production and some buses were beginning to sound slightly breathless.

Recertification of KSW6Bs was not an option, solid though these buses were. The integral Bristol LS single-deckers were almost as old, presenting their own problems with terminally corroded sub-frames. A perfect storm was brewing, with no silver lining in sight.

Fortunately for United Counties, a solution was found. Some other National Bus Company (NBC) operators had already rid themselves of K-types and were selling off Lodekkas by 1971. These were often Gardner-engined, and by then United Counties' FS6Gs had redeemed themselves and were now regarded as the Rolls-Royces of the fleet.

Among the first acquisitions was a pair of 14-year-old LD6Gs from Cumberland, 946/7 (UAO 376/8). They were rushed down to Luton to replace the ailing ex-corporation stock; their open platforms were no problem on intensive Luton town services and they were quick off the block with their low-speed differentials.

On the other hand, 948/9 (LFW 320/3), 1955 LD6Bs from Lincolnshire, were endowed with platform doors and five-speed gearboxes, so they went to Bedford where they proved ideal for country runs. As more buses arrived, Luton with its hilly terrain tended to get the slightly more powerful Gardners, just as in earlier times K6Bs predominated over less-powerful Gardner 5LW-engined K5Gs.

The new normal

Before long, it became business as usual to see secondhand arrivals passing through Northampton central works, some of which sat more comfortably in the fleet than others.

The LDs from Western National, Lincolnshire, Cumberland, Red & White and Southern Vectis were almost indistinguishable from United Counties standard fare, whereas the Midland General group's take on details such as destination equipment and seating added variations on the Lodekka theme.

The Brighton, Hove & District Lodedkka FSFs lent their own quirkiness to the mix – Beetonson vents, metal slats over the windows, and – albeit over-painted – side route number boxes. Crosville supplied the last LDs delivered to a Tilling company, 576-9 (620-3 LFM), 1960 incarnations with Cave-Browne-Cave heating and inadequate hopper vents.

From Southern Vectis came nine 1954 Lodekka LD6Gs of 1954. These were low-mileage and in excellent condition, having spent numerous winters delicensed as operations on the Isle of Wight were highly seasonal. Their open platforms and low-speed differentials made them ideal for intensive and hilly Luton town services. This is 936 (KDL 407), turning at Wandon Close, Stopsley.

Mileage was still being lost because of vehicle shortages throughout 1973, despite the elimination of the Luton Corporation double-deckers and the last KSWs. Another solution was sought — help from operators in a strong enough position to send buses on loan. Soon, unlikely performers on Northampton, Kettering and Bedford routes were Eastern National's cream Lodekka FLF coaches, including two semi-automatic models whose

United Counties' oldest secondhand Lodekka was ex-Red & White 920 (LAX 624), dating from March 1954 and the first LD6G built. This was how it looked at the end of five years' hard graft on Luton town service. Despite their age, the LAXs survived to be among the last LDs withdrawn, in 1976. The home-made replacement grille has FS parentage.

ABOVE: *The need for new buses is graphically illustrated in a busy Luton town centre in 1974. Lodekka LD6B 993 (MNV 110), dating from 1956, was only a few months away from scrapping, while another native LD6B is in the background.*

BELOW: *Desperate times. Marshall-bodied Leyland Leopard 231 (DUC 70C), acquired with Birch Bros' Rushden-London services in 1969, helps out on the Northampton-Wellingborough corridor, but is unable to show route information. These busy routes were normally double-decked and an FLF Lodekka behind the Leopard is about to reverse on to the bay, to the relief of the queue of passengers. The 1930s Art Deco Derngate bus station would in three years become a memory, along with the excursion boards and red telephone box.*

shrieking transmission set dogs howling and may have contravened the Noise Abatement Act.

Red Lodekkas from West Yorkshire and Cumberland added colour to the fleet – these were sensibly kept away from Northampton with its similarly-coloured municipal fleet, although an errant Cumberland LD sometimes found its way in from Corby. Among the melee, an LD from West Yorkshire (TWY 609) was even painted green, rumoured to have been mistaken for an acquired bus. No harm was done (apart from the waste of paint), since the West Yorkshire buses went straight for scrap at the end of their tenure without returning home.

Diversity transformed the fleet as Maidstone & District lent some dark green AEC Reliance single-deckers, while Trent sent cream and red Leyland Tiger Cubs to join five that were purchased from East Yorkshire. Passengers at bus stops must have wondered what apparition would turn up. But this was the 1970s, a time of strikes, power cuts, bus and crew shortages...so maybe they thought this was the new normal and were simply grateful that something actually came along.

Anything that moved

In its search for secondhand vehicles, United Counties appeared to consider anything

that moved, including three slightly dubious Cumberland early LD6Gs, 580-2 (ORM 136/44, RAO 728), the last of which was deemed too poor to use.

By contrast, nine Southern Vectis LD6Gs, KDL 402-410 wearing KSWs' dead men's shoes fleetnumbers 931-9, were in excellent fettle. After a well-maintained existence on the Isle of Wight, much of it spent delicensed for the winter months, mileages were low. All but 939 retained their original long apron fronts, and in a nice touch, United Counties reupholstered the seats with correct-style Tilling crisscross pre-1955 moquette.

Pretty soon, most of the network was visited by secondhand stock, but if you liked Lodekka LDs – and I certainly did – Luton was the place to be, with an impressive 49 allocated. It was not a cheap day out from Northampton, though, since no Rover tickets were available. I hope the financially-challenged United Counties of 1974 appreciated my multiple ticket purchases.

It was particularly poignant to ride again on those ex Southern Vectis KDLs, which used to pop up everywhere on my Isle of Wight holidays. That purposeful, reassuring six-cylinder Gardner cackle still echoed from their exhausts as they made short work of Luton's hills, just as they did tackling St Boniface Down. For a while, they gleamed in the shiny coat of NBC green they never received on the Garden Isle, but they soon acquired scrapes that Vectis drivers reputedly would have touched up discreetly with their own little pot of green paint. Another of my quarries was sweet-sounding but work-shy pre-production LD6B 950 (JBD 955).

Lodekka LD6G 584 (VAO 383), hired from Cumberland and operated in its Tilling red livery, helping out on Bedford town service 101, its crew wearing summer jackets. Fourteen years later, ex-London Routemasters ran on this route, painted green.

As fellow NBC operators further advanced their fleet replacement, Lodekka FS6Gs, a raucous-sounding Cumberland FLF6LX (appropriately registered BRM) and another Brighton & Hove FSF made the pilgrimage to the central works to be repainted and rushed into service. My cycle ride home from school was enlivened by revelations almost every day; what would appear next? Making

Willowbrook-bodied Bedford YRT 123 (LVV 123P), one of the last to arrive in March 1976, in the Northamptonshire countryside when new with driver Ray Walton at the wheel.

United Counties' last Lodekka LDs were withdrawn in 1976, but its problems were not over. The condition of the FS6Bs and FLF6Bs was deteriorating, exacerbated by the lack of spares for their engines. The troublesome Cave-Browne-Cave heating was given to boiling, as is evident in this view of 671 (CNV 671B) steaming towards Luton from Bedford shortly before withdrawal.

close acquaintance with the new arrivals was no problem, since in those days I could wander unchallenged around the site, assuming the innocent persona of a gricer, notebook in hand, camera poised.

Meanwhile, the Eastern National FLF coaches settled in, providing unexpected luxury and speed on longer routes (five-speed gearboxes were never specified on United Counties double-deckers), while the Maidstone & District Reliances sent vintage AEC sounds mewing round the streets of Bedford, alongside red Lodekka LDs and FSs from West Yorkshire Road Car. Could the scene become any more varied?

Odd sounds, odd placenames
The replacement of seven-year-old Dennis Lolines with 17-year-old Lodekkas made sense; a lot more sense than the allocation of three Albion Lowlanders to "pure" United Counties depots.

Northampton received 837 (177 HTM), so it was just possible, for a limited time, to hear their Leyland clunks and gurgles — interspersed by the savage hissing of air-operated sliding doors – in the likes of Buttock's Booth, Husband's Bosworth and Lumbertubs. Universally hated by crews (though

highly entertaining to enthusiasts), they posed additional problems with their single-track number blinds.

Aylesbury received 827 (167 HTM), while 825 (165 HTM) went to Corby where routes were numbered in the 200s, so the prefix "2" was painted on to its bodywork. Luton's LD6Bs were being cascaded to other depots at the time, so why were another three not included in the re-allocations?

Of the borrowed buses, the most bizarre were six of Northampton Corporation's Roe-bodied Daimler CVG6s, though they never actually made it into service with United Counties; 228-30/2 (ONH 228-30/2) of 1962 and 234/5 (RNH 234/5) of 1963 were driven to Kettering depot and even had their destination screens masked down to receive standard United Counties spidery one-line displays. Open platforms, full-height bodies and preselector gearboxes all conspired against them. The hapless Daimlers skulked their way back to Northampton, never to be used in service again. I would have loved to see one accidentally painted green.

The secondhand stock generally served United Counties well. The stars were the Red & White LD6Gs acquired in 1971, 920-5 (LAX 624-9), which reached an impressive age of 22 years on Luton's punishing town services; they were even repainted into NBC green in 1975. LAX 624 incidentally was the first Gardner-engined Lodekka built, in March 1954.

Were it not for United Counties, it is likely much of the acquired stock would otherwise have gone for scrap. Dealer Hartwood Finance was an assiduous buyer of anything with a 6LW at the time, since these engines were in demand for export — some are probably still chugging away in Chinese junks.

Meanwhile, some operators were allegedly so determined that their perfectly sound withdrawn buses would see no further use by competitors that they set about their engines with sledgehammers or poured sand down the filler caps. The 1970s were indeed strange times.

The lightweight at the end of the tunnel
The great invasion could never be more than a stopgap. United Counties, like some other operators, looked beyond British Leyland for new vehicles, and the unlikely saviours were Willowbrook-bodied Bedford YRQ and YRT single-deckers, purchased from 1974.

Cheap and cheerful, they reduced the average age of the fleet markedly, took pressure off the engineering department, increased one-person operation and modernised the company image, all in one fell swoop. Not that they could ever rival the longevity of the Lodekkas, but they got the company out of a hole. Seven years was the usual lifespan of these Bedfords; the Red & White LDs achieved over three times that innings.

The Bedford/Willowbrooks were more pleasant on the eye than the ear, and not popular with drivers who had hoped manual gearboxes were on the way out. One wag compared gear changing in a Bedford to stirring soup with a knitting needle, and the unfortunate grating and crunching of gears that echoed around Derngate bus station was frequently followed by a painful shuddering as a driver resorted to taking off in any forward gear he could lay his hand on.

Around 50 Bedfords were purchased, and their entry into service by summer 1976 almost exactly mirrored the departure of the secondhand Lodekkas and native LDs,.

Meanwhile, deliveries of new Bristol VRs and Leyland Nationals gained pace. Just as well, since spares for the BVW units in FSs and FLFs had also gone out of production, presenting another headache for the company. Many of these hapless late-model Lodekkas also had the dreaded Cave-Browne-Cave heating system.

Breakdowns were not uncommon. One FS6B expired near Northampton, 10miles into its journey to Barnsley dealers, and another added excitement to my ride from Bedford to Luton by suddenly cutting out halfway up a hill.

Over 100 VRs materialised between 1973 and 1979, accompanied by more than 50 Leyland Nationals.

The last FS6Bs and FLF6Bs went in 1980, leaving the excellent FS6Gs to soldier on briefly as the company's last halfcabs...until, in Stagecoach ownership, a fleet of ex-London Routemasters swept into service in Bedford and Corby, but that is another story.

Plus ça change

A break from my French studies in 1981 brought me home to Northampton by way of a 50mile winter's ride on United Counties route 128 — ten years after shivering on a KSW.

But the interminable 2hr or so on the top deck of Bristol VRT/SL2 759 (VNV 759H) was a freezing cold endurance test; the seating consisted of unyielding and clammy dark green Vynide, the interior all clinical plastic and fluorescent lighting, and the driver of 759 flicked his way from first to fourth gear in just a few seconds, foot steadfastly on the accelerator, before settling at a mind-numbing snail's pace. Bus design had progressed since the 1950s...scheduling, driving standards and passenger comfort less so.

Consider this. In 1971, United Counties had well over 200 double-deckers in its fleet with Bristol engines, yet all were replaced within nine years. The company's recovery was a remarkable one, in no short measure thanks to its resilience and resourcefulness, and a dogged determination not to take the easy option and simply slash fleet size and withdraw routes.

Happier days lay ahead, but the departure of the last halfcabs, and the resulting sea of leaf green VRs and riveted — but not riveting — Leyland Nationals left me cold, and I sought excitement elsewhere. ■

Sunnier days ahead. United Counties bravely enters the new decade with a double-deck fleet composed almost entirely of Bristol VRs. Series 3 model 879 (XNV 879S) speeds its way to Northampton from Wellingborough in July 1980.

Stagecoach acquired former Alder Valley 1509 (B577 LPE), new 1985, when it acquired the Cleveland Transit business on Teesside in October 1994. It had been re-registered PJI 4983 by then and was transferred north the following year to the Western Buses fleet. This shows it leaving Glasgow's Buchanan bus station on the all-stops route to Ayr. That service still runs today, but is complemented by motorway express journeys operated mainly with modern double-deck coaches.

Olympian coaches

The deregulation of services carrying passengers making journeys of 30miles or longer from October 1980 was a spur for the development of services into London from surrounding towns, especially for commuters dissatisfied by rail travel.

To meet demand and avoid running duplicate coaches, between 1983 and 1986 four National Bus Company subsidiaries bought a new long-wheelbase version of the Leyland Olympian announced in 1982 when a prototype was delivered to National Travel, complete with a restyled body built by Leyland's Eastern Coach Works (ECW) factory in Lowestoft.

The ONTL11/2RSp was 11.2m (36ft 8in) long with a 6,528mm (21ft 5in) wheelbase. Its 245hp Leyland TL11 engine was coupled to a five-speed Hydracyclic gearbox. The body used the structure of the standard ECW bus body, but with a raked upper deck windscreen.

London Country bought 15 as its LRC class for Green Line services, Maidstone & District took 14 for Invictaway routes from the Medway Towns, while ten each went to Alder Valley (for Londonlink) and Eastern National. Most were

We complete our pictorial review of 1980s Leylands with the long-wheelbase ECW-bodied Olympian coaches built mainly for London commuter services, but photographed in later life in Scotland by **BILLY NICOL**

This was another of the Alder Valley coaches, new in 1983 as 1503 (YPJ 503Y). It had gained some front end styling embellishment, and cherished registration 341 AYF, when the Clyde Coast business in Ayrshire owned it from 1991 to 1992.

14ft 2in high, but the Eastern National ten were 13ft 8in to meet its lowheight requirement.

In addition to these, ECW restyled the body in 1984 to look more like a coach, but only 20 were built, 13 of them for export.

The 49 London commuter vehicles led short lives in their original roles, especially once the NBC subsidiaries were privatised, but most were either transferred to other ex-NBC fleets — such as Northumbria — or were sold to third party buyers attracted by their potentially high seating capacity. Several of them eventually reached Scottish fleets through a variety of routes. ■

British Bus transferred 13 of the Olympian coaches to its Clydeside fleet in 1996, with 899 (C449 BKM) — in Paisley on the main corridor route into Glasgow — coming from Northumbria. It had been new to Maidstone & District in 1985 as its 5449.

Strathclyde Buses purchased four of these vehicles — three new to London Country, one to Maidstone & District — from Northumbria in 1995 for its low-cost GCT unit. They remained after First acquired the employee-owned Strathclyde business the following year, with the GCT operation integrated into what became First Glasgow. LO105 (C211 UPD) was new to London Country in 1986 as its LRC11.

Crews on **parade**

DAVID PIKE recalls when most buses had a conductor as well as a driver, something that lasted much longer on one route in one modest-sized city

Many readers will have encountered bus crews who dislike appearing in a photograph, but many others pose happily with their steed to create a classic pose.

Take, for example, the crew of Leicester City Transport 246 (FUT 246V), an East Lancs-bodied Dennis Dominator, in 1982. Leicester has long been multi-cultural city and this driver was of Pakistani heritage and the conductress Irish.

The conductor's Ultimate ticket machine was weighty because it contained six ticket rolls, and the system was expensive to administer, as the issue of numbered ticket rolls had to be audited. But it operated swiftly on busy urban services and a wide range of fares could be accommodated by issuing double or combination tickets.

In 1984, 30miles away, Northampton Transport 261 (GNH 261F) was one of three Roe-bodied Daimler CVG6s left in the fleet. Two were required for diagrams that included Links View service 13 with its reverse at the Pioneer pub.

The spare bus, turning here at Southfields and crewed by former London Transport conductress Gloria Cowling with me at the wheel (and photographed by Laurence Knight), covered one-person duties like route 9 via Semilong, its traditional Five Bells terminus in Kingsthorpe and industrial estates and the Southfields residential estate to the north. The Almex ticket machines used in Northampton were lighter and more flexible than the Ultimates they replaced.

Elsewhere in Northamptonshire, Kevin Lane captured Michael Hedge emerging from the depths of United Counties' Wellingborough garage in July 1979 to join conductor Charlie Patel with Bristol Lodekka FS6B 651 (651 EBD). Was the garage door very low or the driver very tall? The Tilling architecture of the 1938 building is typical of its era.

Wellingborough operated town and industrial services and the trunk Nene Valley corridor running east from Northampton to Raunds. The depot, which closed in 1986, was regarded as militant because of its reluctance to accept double-deck one-person operation. Possibly as a ruse, manual gearbox vehicles were not accepted for one-person work and the depot (along with Luton) received none of the large delivery of Bedford single-deckers so equipped in the mid-1970s. By way of punishment, an early allocation of crew-worked Bristol VRTs was moved elsewhere.

Wellingborough could still muster eight Lodekka FSs and seven FLFs but no VRTs among its 32-vehicle allocation at the end of 1976. Lodekkas still outnumbered VRTs three years later.

Crews are often proud of a new bus, particularly when it is a new model. Such pride is evident in the view above from my collection, taken at Portland Bill, where despite the 'Jack Harper' jaunty cap and stance of the conductor. Southern National took delivery of its first modern looking Bristol RELLs in 1967. They entered service at Weymouth with conductors on the complex Isle of Portland 22 group of services, but were soon converted to one-person operation and dispersed elsewhere, notably to Seaton for the 213 service from there to Taunton.

All part of the service for rural independents

Dorset Queen Coaches operated about a dozen vehicles from the village of Chaldon near Lulworth Cove on schools, private hire, contract work and tours, and also a traditional Wednesday market day and Saturday service into Dorchester.

On August 27, 1980, a nearly new and smartly turned out Plaxton Supreme-bodied Bedford YMT (XAA 27V) was about to leave Dorchester with a healthy load. Although a conductor was not strictly necessary, some private firms valued the more personal service a crew of two provided.

The Dorset Queen business survived in the same family until 2004 but the successor, Hookways of Devon, closed the Chaldon base the following year. Today the main bus service in the area, First X54, is focused more on traffic between centres such as Weymouth, Wool, Wareham and Poole than any custom from small villages. Timetables such as that operated by Dorset Queen are largely a thing of the past.

WEBB, M. H. (Dorset Queen Coaches), East Chaldon, DORCHESTER
Tel. Warmwell 852829

DORCHESTER - LULWORTH COVE
Weekdays

Summer work for 60s and 70s students

Bus conducting was a well-paid and enjoyable job for students, particularly in the late 1960s and early 1970s, and staff shortages ensured that such work was readily available even in non-holiday towns. Opportunities were much more limited by the 1980s, but Southern Vectis still employed a significant number of seasonal staff on the Isle of Wight.

Full uniforms were often not issued to short-term staff. This gave rise to the trainers, jeans and T-shirt complemented by a National Bus Company summer jacket 'student' look which the young can get away with. In this September 1983 view at the Cowes terminus of the trunk service 1 to Newport and Ryde, the youthful crew of Bristol VRT 660 (CDL 660R) that David Ferguson photographed are working a 1B variation.

Possibly not a student, but another youthful conductor awaits custom for a Weymann-bodied AEC Regent V typical of the South Wales fleet, at Llanelli in September 1976. Before the NBC territorial changes in the area, the route as service 2 had been a joint South Wales and United Welsh operation. The advertisements for colour television rental are a reminder that colour was still new and many people rented rather than owned what would be the only set in their home.

Illustrating the situation in west Wales before the territorial changes is St Davids-based AEC Renown 730 (DBO 730C) at Haverfordwest railway station in 1968. Its crew bask in the morning summer sun before setting off for home. Route 802 had its origins in a Great Western Railway service and ran roughly

hourly. All three of these smart Northern Counties-bodied Renowns were first allocated to St Davids.

The depot closed within three years and the route was withdrawn as part of wholesale service cuts by Western Welsh in Pembrokeshire. Coincidentally, the Cardiff-based Hancocks brewery advertised on the front of the bus was taken over by Bass in 1968 and, a bit like the bus industry, that brand underwent several subsequent changes of ownership.

Dual crews were perfectly okay for OK at Bishop Auckland

The advent of rear-engined buses did not always herald conversion to one-person operation, even in later years.

OVK 136M, rounding the Market Place on the town service in Bishop Auckland in summer 1983, was one of six 1973 Alexander-bodied Leyland Atlantean AN68s that OK Motor Services bought when they were less than ten years old.

The service operated to a tight 30min schedule with one bus, something unachievable without the use of a dual crew as it was termed in north-east. Lily Etherington, standing on the platform, worked the service for most of the day six days a week and was well-known in the town.

An earlier bargain for OK was its purchase of seven former Southdown Leyland Titan PD3s with Northern Counties 'Queen Mary' bodywork. By the summer of 1982, when PD3 BUF 279C was in the care of driver Michael Greig and conductor Arthur Bayles at Evenwood, the use of such buses on service work was largely confined to summer Saturdays when more modern vehicles were required for working men's club trips to the likes of Whitley Bay.

By contrast, and in 1976, a slightly battered United Bristol Lodekka FSF6B 268 (2068 HN) rests in Bishop Auckland Market Place on town route 9, which covered much the same area of Bishop as

OK's but by a different route and more frequently. With a round trip running only a shade over 20min, the United driver is probably pondering on his pipe that he has several more to go before the end of his shift.

Busy buses, particularly in the central belt, meant that some Scottish Bus Group (SBG) companies were slow to dispense with conductors. Indeed, the group disposed of Bristol VRTs capable of being operated without a conductor in the early 1970s in exchange for crew-worked Lodekka FLFs from the National Bus Company.

In Edinburgh, although the last FLFs were withdrawn in June 1982, crew operation on the busy Dalkeith corridor continued briefly with Daimler Fleetlines. The conductor who has just alighted from ECW-bodied DD504 (BSG 504L) of 1973 is modelling a 'low apron' Setright at the St Andrew Square bus station in Edinburgh.

Single-deckers operated what was expected at the time to be the last SBG crew-operated service, the Eastern Scottish Linlithgow (F) allocation on the Edinburgh-Stirling service 38. Alexander-bodied Seddon Pennine 7 S633 (YSG 633W), photographed by David Ferguson, makes a crew change (far left) at the Linlithgow mid-point.

While sturdy and reliable, the Seddons were not blessed with a low floor; the parking, rather distant

from the kerb, probably did not raise eyebrows then in the way it would today. Passengers could board their crew-operated bus at leisure without waiting for a fare-collecting driver to set up.

That was 1982, when nobody would surely have predicted that crew operation would return to SBG within three years. With the new Clydeside fleet in the vanguard followed by Kelvin, Routemasters with conductors were deployed in and around

Glasgow and also in Perth and Dundee with the Strathtay company.

The main Dundee RM route was a cross-city operation which to the east extended up the coast to Carnoustie. The route to the west was not so lengthy, although RMs crossed the Tay Bridge for a time. When this photograph was taken on August 31, 1993 near the end of Routemaster operation, the western terminus was on the north bank of the Tay at Kingoodie where driver Angus Mackenzie and his Setright-bearing conductor posed for Ian Manning.

The demise of Routemasters outside London, largely in the 1990s, heralded a return to one-person operation, but not in Dundee.

Competition with Travel Dundee's exact fare buses, and running times that could be worked with fewer buses when crew operated, resulted in Strathtay retaining conductors. The route was extended farther up the coast to Arbroath and in a reversal of past practice where buses carried signs to show they were one-person operated, these carried a 'conductor on board' logo.

Other than on heritage services, crew operation in London ceased in 2005, but it was not until March 2020 and a full 40 years after many places in the UK that the Dundee conductors hung up their cash bags for the last time. The Covid pandemic precluded the use of perambulating conductors and passenger numbers were depleted significantly too.

Their employment was suspended and Stagecoach confirmed in September 2020 that they would not return. The 31 staff were either redeployed or made redundant. Thus a significant chapter in British bus history, largely unrecognised outside Dundee, closed without notice or ceremony. David Jenkins's pictures taken in 2019 illustrate the strange sight of a conductor aboard an Alexander Dennis Enviro400 MMC-bodied Volvo B5LH hybrid. ■

Victoria Park Cardiff trolleybus terminus with 1948 East Lancs-bodied BUT 214 making the tight turn in April 1968 shortly before the conversion to motorbuses. The six minute frequency was replaced by one of 20 minutes. The photographer is at Timbuktu. MIKE RUSSELL

Voyages of colourful discovery

ROGER DAVIES looks back fondly to the 1960s and the varied bus scenes he explored on his home turf of south Wales and soon afterwards across urban Yorkshire

In February 1950, Cardiff was finally rid of its clapped out tramcars, replaced by a fleet of modern, sleek trolleybuses. Two months later I arrived on the scene at my grandparents' house and lived for the next 18 years near the Victoria Park trolley terminus.

Here the old trams had dumped people in the middle of the road and to continue westwards to the big Ely estate, people had to change on to motorbuses. It amazes me that, to this day, transport planners think it a good idea to turf people off one vehicle and change on to another. If it is to be a suitable alternative to the car, public transport should offer a direct journey for as many as possible, what is known in the United States as a "one seat rode".

The motorbuses congregated around an island with an odd wooden shelter. We lived with my grandparents, Fred and Gin. Gin had a way with words and to signify something as being a long way away used to refer to it as "like going to Timbuktu". In my young mind that bus shelter was like Timbuktu.

At first trolleybuses on the 5/A/B and 8 terminated there, but in 1955 wires were extended to well over twice their length with the new 10A/B routes to Ely, the only significant trolleybus extension beyond the old tramway. This gave us 32 trolleybuses an hour plus a few motorbuses.

Terminating trolleybuses used a very tight turning circle requiring two manually operated frogs, meaning conductors had to skip around what was the busy main westward A48 out of the city. Years later, I discovered one idea would have had them running around my house. I would never have left home.

A perfect interchange

Cardiff is unusually blessed with a main railway station that is convenient for the city centre. In the early 1950s a bus station was built opposite it, thus not only offering bus/rail connections but also being handy for the majority of bus users who had no need of such a thing. A happy arrangement that local politicians, usually the first to bang on about interchange, seemed to forget and felt a new office for the BBC was better than a bus station. Odd for a bus company-owning council

In its heyday, the bus station was a mecca for local and visiting enthusiasts. While it did not house all corporation services, some were on the other side of the centre in Greyfriars Road, many did and trolleybuses passed by. And what a mecca it was. Other municipal operators came in on joint services, all with their own ideas on livery and bus types.

Green and cream Newport buses came on the joint service from there with Cardiff, now the last remaining joint service run by municipals. Dark maroon West Mon and dark green and cream Caerphilly buses came in on the mighty joint 36 with Cardiff to Tredegar. Merthyr provided maroon buses on the service thereto joint with Cardiff and Rhondda. They called it the 7 but did not use route

Newport had a varied fleet but was dominated by Longwell Green-bodied Leyland Titan PD2/40s like 61 dating from 1959. In May 1972 it is passing the castle, showing Newport's habit of identifying circular services either with C for clockwise or A for anticlockwise. GEOFFREY MORANT

numbers, Cardiff the 20 (formerly 41) and Rhondda the 100. Nobody seemed confused.

An easy bus ride away could be found the municipal fleets of Pontypridd in dark blue and cream, Aberdare in a racy cream with almost lilac bands, blue and cream Bedwas & Machen and the striking green, red and grey of Gelligaer. But do not go there; its buses congregated at Hengoed.

BET was well represented by the mid-red of Western Welsh, which was based in the city, and the darker red of Rhondda. From 1965, Western Welsh added to the colour palette with blue and cream coaches and dual-purpose buses, Rhondda following suit with green and cream.

Then there was the stunning Neath & Cardiff, its brown and red coaches whizzing off to Swansea had pole position at the exit to the bus station. It was a common meeting point — "See you at the N&C" — for a night out in the city.

There was a state-owned company, Red & White, but its standard fare in Tilling red was overshadowed by the variety of others, although some interesting pre-state ownership stuff remained. After the opening of the Severn Bridge in 1966, they were joined by Tilling greens from Bristol. There were regular visits on express coach services from Black & White, Midland Red and Crosville, the latter usually in cream and black.

Unlike other parts of south Wales, few independents ran into Cardiff. The main one was Thomas of Barry which shared the 304 route there via Dinas Powis with Western Welsh, a run known to their crews as the "low road". The "top road" was the 303 via Wenvoe.

A trip westwards would take you via Port Talbot with its striking petrol blue buses of BET's Thomas Bros to Swansea. While this was home to Tilling red United Welsh, originally an offshoot of Red & White, it was dominated by the BET fleet of South Wales in its deep red. This was a truly fabulous fleet which was virtually the operating arm of the AEC catalogue.

It is interesting to take an overview along the Severn Estuary. There were the urban fleets of BET in Swansea, municipals in Cardiff and Newport and Tilling in Bristol, all very different.

Cardiff Corporation was interesting in itself with a varied fleet in crimson lake and cream . In addition to the joint services mentioned earlier, it ran jointly with Western Welsh to nearby Penarth on the coast, with summer extensions to Lavernock. Originally this required single-deckers but a new road missing

In blue and cream, Western Welsh 1966 Marshall-bodied Leyland Tiger Cub 1379 is on the sort of joint route with Cardiff, the 333 going beyond the corporation's 33. It is at the ideally located Cardiff bus station in September 1969. ROY MARSHALL/ THE BUS ARCHIVE

the offending bridge at Cog solved this and Cardiff's nine single-deckers spent a lot of time on the forecourt of Sloper Road depot.

Another sort of joint route went to Radyr and Morganstown, but the Western Welsh bit, a 333 rather than 33, went farther to Church Village Most interesting of all was Cardiff's own 32 which wandered out through the Vale of Glamorgan, Cardiff's stockbroker belt, for about 10miles to Hensol, a mental institution.

These out-of-city routes were usually home to some unusual Alexander-bodied Crossleys, later replaced by rather exotic AEC Bridgemasters that had platform doors.

Cardiff had five main bus depots. Red & White had a small one in Gelligaer Street behind Maindy sports stadium. This hosted school sports days, and the depot offered a nice escape route from the horrors perpetuated in the stadium. The Western Welsh head office and central works was at Ely and a visit there usually resulted in a friendly guided tour of this extensive and interesting facility.

The other three constituted my usual Saturday morning outing. I would take an 8 trolleybus to Royal Oak terminus right across the city then walk to Cardiff Corporation's Roath depot on Newport Road. This was the trolleybus depot but from 1962

also housed replacement diesels. It was also a sort of central works so motorbuses in various states of repair could be found.

The route past the depot, the 2, had been the first to be converted so the depot was out on a limb at the eastern edge of the system. A bus ride back to the bus station allowed that to be checked out.

A walk down Penarth Road allowed a visit to the local Western Welsh operating depot which would later be the start of my National Bus Company career. It was also home to six N&C coaches denoted by a white triangle on the front . A walk through Grangetown took in the corporation's Sloper Road depot, the main motorbus base. A final walk home finished off some extensive bus enthusiasm involving a fair amount of exercise.

Surely this was normal

The main point of all this was that, for me, this was perfectly normal, how I assumed buses were in all places. My first substantial visit outside south Wales did nothing to disabuse this notion.

It was to West Yorkshire. We had relatives in Bradford and in 1965 drove up to stay with them. In those pre-motorway days this required an overnight stop in Shrewsbury. The first day was pretty uneventful, day two very different. We got to the environs of Stockport and the red and cream buses of BET's North Western, including the remarkable lowheight Dunham Massey Bedford VALs.

Over the Pennines we arrived in Huddersfield, with the fabulous trolleybus network still in evidence. And then on to Bradford. Oddly, the wonderful Bud Morgan's model shop in Cardiff only stocked two *British Bus Fleets* books, our local 18, South Wales, and 2, Yorkshire municipals. So I was pretty well up on the Bradford fleet.

But it was striking how the bright blue and cream buses really lifted the city. Yes there were lots of trolleybuses. Wherever you drove in the city, you seemed to cross wiring. And thanks to extensive rebodying, they looked modern. But for me the huge fleet of front-entrance MCW-bodied AEC Regent Vs was the real shock. These were buses used by BET companies Rhondda and South Wales and to my eyes decidedly exciting and un-municipal.

In 1966, I returned on my own by train just after the release of the Beatles *Revolver* album, changing at Manchester. In 1967 I went by coach, changing at Birmingham. From 1968 until 1972, I was in college in Sheffield which meant regular visits to Bradford for my aunt to do my washing.

A fun visit for everyone

The 1966 visit was fun. After crossing the viaduct at Stockport with lots of red and cream corporation buses below me, I was met by assorted cousins in Manchester and whisked quickly across the city centre to make a connection. There were hordes of red Manchester Corporation buses, various others, a glimpse of a blue Ashton trolleybus then, to my amazement, a bus station chock-a-block full of green Salford buses.

Among this abundance of buses I thought it must be really helpful to people to have different coloured buses to find the right one. Manchester was surely the spiritual home of route branding that became so successful years later.

By some subterfuge, likely suggesting young ladies could not resist a man who could tell a Fleetline from an Atlantean, I had got my similar age cousin interested in buses and we spent a happy time visiting nearby centres. Nearby Leeds with its very dark green buses showed a totally different approach. Despite some rear-engined types and five front-entrance Daimler CVG6s to match Bradford's fare on the joint 72 between the cities, it remained wedded to rear-entrance double-deckers, lots of the AECs but a pretty good mix.

After many years of storming Bradford's hills including on the 85, 1949 Leyland-bodied Titan PD2/3 568 became training bus 034. It is at Hall Ings during April 1967. GEOFFREY MORANT

Halifax was another to have front-entrance AEC Regent Vs, but this one dating from 1964 with Weymann body was ex-Hebble. Much of the Hebble operation was absorbed into Halifax forming Calderdale in 1971. No.312, formerly Hebble 316, is in the striking and cheery Halifax livery on a former Hebble service at the town's general hospital in April 1974. DON AKRIGG

West Riding's front-engined Guy Wulfrunians came in several hues. Red was used for former Wakefield tram routes from where the company originated, green for the rest of the fleet. Early models had more cream changing to red or green with cream window surrounds as here, finally ending up in green with a cream band as on the one behind. Roe-bodied 957 of 1963 is at Wakefield in September 1968. JOHN KAYE

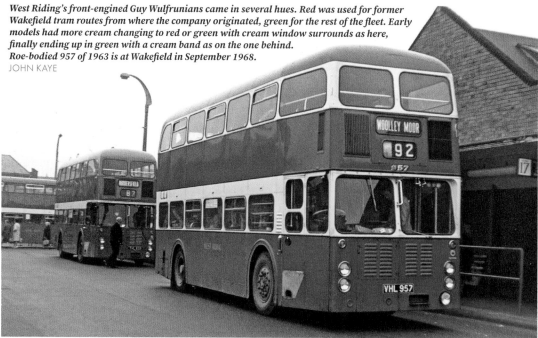

A 64 in the other direction brought you to Huddersfield with its smart red and cream buses. And here was the first of a strange phenomenon of the area, joint omnibus committees. Here, services in the urban area were provided by the corporation, the A fleet, those to outlying areas by a joint board with British Railways, the B fleet.

This meant that services I would have expected to be run by local company operators had sort of corporation buses on them. I say sort of, as in

Sheffield's fabulously impractical livery gave the city a distinct character. Weymann-bodied AEC Regent V 449, new in 1960, passes Fitzalan Square in 1969 on service 60, the only one to start outside Midland station. ROY MARSHALL/ THE BUS ARCHIVE

Huddersfield, the true corporation buses had the cream sweeping down to cover the whole of the lower front under the windscreen, while joint buses had merely three cream bands which I felt gave a most impressive appearance.

Another giveaway was that for many years corporation buses were all trolleybuses, giving the town the finest system of such things with its numerous hills. By my time, these were giving way to motorbuses, Leyland Titan PD3s and Daimler CVG6s on which the cream front around the engine looked odd and impractical.

And then there was Halifax, another with a joint omnibus committee. Here there was no livery differentiation; all were in the splendid, striking, cheerful, green orange and cream, only the fleetnumber giving the game away.

Nestled among them all was Todmorden, another joint board. The very standardised fleet of Leyland Titan PD2s in dark green and cream was split between the corporation and BR, carrying appropriate logos. It will always be special for me as cousin John and I peered into the depot at Millwood we were cordially invited in and given a tour.

But just because there were these odd joint boards did not mean there were no area company operators. Far from it, there were loads of them. A

favourite was BET's Hebble based in Halifax with around 80 buses in an agreeable darkish red and cream, many of them AECs including familiar front-entrance Regent Vs.

They seemed to sneak though suburbs, popping up in unusual places, but were party with Bradford and Huddersfield on the 64 between the two places. In Huddersfield could be found the cream and blue BET County Motors fleet based near the Waterloo trolleybus terminus. Much larger were the two BETs of Yorkshire Traction, its mid-red and cream buses hailing from Barnsley, and Yorkshire Woollen in a rather drab overall red coming from Dewsbury.

Treated to a variety

Which brings us to location. My relatives lived in Low Moor and we were treated to a variety of buses, all of which would take us to the city centre. Bradford's 85 to Oakenshaw was usually provided by Leyland-bodied Titans from Bankfoot depot which was passed on the way.

Then there was the mighty 66 from Sheffield, including shorts to Dewsbury numbered 65. This was operated jointly by Traction and Woollen along with Sheffield Transport. The latter was even more fascinating in not only having A and B fleets, but a

C fleet wholly owned by British Railways which ran very long services like the 66 and ones to the Peak District, Manchester and Gainsborough.

It was not too choosy about allocating buses and I once rode a new A fleet Neepsend-bodied Atlantean for the local ride in Bradford, something I found very interesting.

Tracky tended towards its favoured Northern Counties-bodied PD3s but Woollen often used Leyland Tigers rebodied as double-deckers mainly with MCW Orion bodies. But one batch really confused me. These had Roe front-entrance bodies with mod cons like fluorescent lighting, but retained their old registrations which were two letters, HD, and four numbers.

What made a lot of this amazing is that the routes climbed all the way out of Bradford, the 66 starting at Chester Street bus station, did not even make it to the flat. Yet both Bradford Corporation and Woollen used pretty ancient quite standard buses on what was gruelling work. Woollen was one of BET's money spinners, so perhaps being frugal with buses helped.

Sometimes some rather ungainly front-entrance tin front PD3s would turn up. It had quite a large fleet of MCW front-entrance Regent Vs but oddly these never seemed to turn up to mix with their brethren in blue.

In Leeds, the dark blue buses of East Yorkshire could also be seen. The state-owned Tilling group was represented by the red West Yorkshire fleet

hailing from Harrogate. Very traditional in its ways, it stuck with rear-entrance 60-seat Bristol Lodekkas right up to 1966.

It had a few interesting twists. It operated in York and Keighley on a joint arrangement with those councils, buses there carrying the placename in front of the fleetname and the fleetnumbers prefaced by Y or K. Keighley ones appeared in Bradford. And its coaches carried an attractive cream and maroon livery which was unusual. One of these took us on a day trip to Blackpool.

Express services brought in other operators such as Ribble. Indeed my ride from Birmingham was on an East Yorkshire Leyland Leopard in its lighter blue coach and dual purpose livery.

Two major independents appeared as well. One of the largest, West Riding, often provided some of its fleet of Guy Wulfrunians in either green or red versions of its livery. And Samuel Ledgard provided a fascinating mix of blue and grey buses, some new but many secondhand including Rochdale AEC Regent IIIs, London RTs and RLHs and ex-South Wales Regent Vs. And Leeds-based Wallace Arnold coaches were much in evidence across West Yorkshire.

Living in Sheffield
In 1968 I went to college in Sheffield and what was one of the UK's most fascinating operators became my local for four years. As we had no halls of residence, I lived in various parts of the city and

Sheffield United Tours' smart livery on 1968 Plaxton Panorama-bodied AEC Reliance 389 is in Derby ROY MARSHALL/THE BUS ARCHIVE

Booth & Fisher had a taste for the Albion Nimbus, This Harrington-bodied 1960 example, originally Western Welsh 14, is at the Halfway depot. ROY MARSHALL/THE BUS ARCHIVE

used the varied fleet widely for all my needs. The striking livery of cream with three blue bands was particularly inspiring and indeed brave.

All these cities still wore the effects of their industrial heritage and the striking, often bright liveries lifted them and gave character. A Sheffield bus emerging from early February morning gloom set you up for the day.

Just because Sheffield Transport itself provided such a wide variety of services did not mean there was no more interest. Other municipals appeared: green and cream Chesterfield, blue and cream Rotherham and red and cream (later purple) Doncaster in addition to Halifax and Huddersfield.

The usual BET suspects could be found, plus the mid-red and creams of North Western and Trent and the deep red of East Midland and the green and cream of Mexborough & Swinton. An interesting BET outfit was coach operator Sheffield United Tours with a smart fleet of red and grey mainly AECs.

Tilling buses were a bit rare, green Lincolnshires came in on the joint with Sheffield 85 to Gainsborough and, by my time, West Riding was state-owned, too but did not yet look like it.

There were still independents. Wigmore of Dinnington had a taste for Bedford VALs in its blue/grey fleet, dark blue Dearneways had a selection of secondhand kit including ex-Western Welsh Leyland Tiger Cubs, and Booth & Fisher's red and cream fleet included some new things but lots of secondhand including Albion Nimbus and Bedford OB.

Given this rich introduction to serious bus enthusiasm, it is hardly surprising I found it difficult to believe there were enthusiasts in places of such dull uniformity as London and Birmingham.

The rot sets in

It was not to last. The rot set in with PTEs. Soon the colourful individualistic Manchester scene became a nondescript sea of identical orange buses, a colour chosen for what it was not rather than what it was. In West Yorkshire, the PTE chose an insipid green and a pale shade called buttermilk with an apologetic logo and the soulless name Metro.

By then all part of the National Bus Company, the company operators reacted by all going poppy red. South Yorkshire PTE took on the world's most unspeakable livery of cream with bits of brown, and again NBC reacted by going poppy red, although green Lincolnshire was still about and, thankfully, East Midland went that way too.

In south Wales, all the shades of red in NBC companies became poppy red and Cardiff went to an NBC-style orange, an image reinforced by a taste for Leyland Nationals and Bristol VRs. Local government reform brought oddities like Rhymney Valley, Islwyn and Taff Ely. The 1970s were a time of service cuts, eye-watering fare increases, depot closures and staff redundancies. Compared with the vibrant 1960s, the 1970s buses seemed to look the depressing part. ∎

Edale is the southern starting point for The Pennine Way, a 268mile footpath running along the hills of the Pennines from end to end and opened in 1965. It is twinned with Kirk Yetholm, the Scottish Borders village at the northern end of the path. Edale has a railway station on the Hope Valley line; bus services have never been its strong point. The Peak District National Park funded a summer leisure service linking the Hope Valley with Blue John Caverns and Derwent Dams. In August of 2019, its first year of operation of the Hope Valley Explorer, Stagecoach Yorkshire Optare Solo 47323 leaves Edale to return to the main road at Hope. Subsequent years saw this section of route omitted to allow a more regular timetable and the use of bigger buses.

Crossing **England's** spine

JOHN YOUNG takes a bus ride along the Pennines and shares some of the sights he has seen at points where services cross this range of hills and mountains

The hills and mountains of the Pennines — the backbone of England — stretch for around 250miles, separating the north-west from Yorkshire and the north-east. They extend northwards from the Peak District, through the South Pennines, Yorkshire Dales and North Pennines to the Tyne Gap, which separates them from the Cheviots. The Eden Valley separates the Pennines from the Lake District mountains.

Although often called a chain, they are broken by many valleys or dales. They form a watershed that determines the course of all the larger rivers in northern England and are broader and generally higher in the north than the south. The highest points are Cross Fell (2,930ft), Whernside (2,419ft), Ingleborough (2,373ft) and Pen-y-Ghent (2,273ft).

The rural Pennine landscape provides urban dwellers with a perfect escape to its fresh air, peace and tranquillity, stunning landscapes, open heather moorlands, dales, rivers and waterfalls, closely knit local communities, attractive stone buildings, birds and wildlife, signs of a mining and industrial past, sheep farming...and buses. The buses provide vital links for the locals but also allow tourists and walkers to access a vast open landscape that may otherwise be off limits.

This snapshot celebrates buses in the Pennine region, with a focus on the more rural elements. The pictures take us in a northerly stroll through this wonderful landscape. Sit back and enjoy the journey. ■

In the southern Pennines, heights of more than 2,000ft are rare. Kinder Scout (2,088ft) is the exception, with Hayfield a popular starting point for walks. This was a mill village from the 17th century. Arthur Lowe, Captain Mainwaring in **Dad's Army**, was born and grew up there. Local bus services are provided by High Peak (to Buxton, Glossop and Macclesfield) and Stagecoach Manchester (to Stockport). High Peak brought together the former Trent Barton Buxton operations and Bowers of Chapel-en-le-Frith. The area was served by the North Western Road Car Company until it was broken up in 1972. A pair of new, short-wheelbase Alexander Dennis Enviro200 MMC were added to the High Peak fleet in March 2022, its first new buses for five years. One of them, 540 (YX22 OGG), arrives at the town's small bus station in April 2022 on an early evening service 61 to Buxton.

Sometimes enthusiasts just happen to be in the right place at the right time. One such occasion was on Sunday December 1, 1985, when South Yorkshire PTE Alexander RH-bodied Dennis Dominator 2462 (C882 JWE) was heading a line-up of three such vehicles travelling east over Woodhead on their delivery run.

The combination of MAN 18.240 chassis and East Lancs Kinetic body was hardly a runaway success. Stagecoach took 16 for its Scottish operations. They were passed on to other group companies, with Yorkshire receiving eight, including 22515 (SF56 FKT) climbing through Hoylandswaine on a journey from Barnsley to Penistone in March 2016. All eight moved subsequently to Stagecoach North East.

The bus route from Holmfirth to Penistone would be a great way to introduce American tourists to the scenic splendour of northern England. Tate's provided the link as service 25 in August 2013. One possible reason for that operator's demise was its provision of some journeys on this thinly populated route on a commercial basis. Optare Solo YJ08 XDH drops down past Winscar Reservoir. TM Travel and South Pennine Community Transport provide the link today.

First Manchester Volvo B9TL/Wright Eclipse Gemini 37553 (MX09 GYF) climbs Standedge in wintry conditions on January 17, 2010. The Great Western Inn opened in 1836 but has since closed. It was named after Brunel's steamship rather than his railway. Service 184 still runs between Huddersfield and Oldham; the Manchester extension was withdrawn. The main Leeds-Manchester railway line runs through a tunnel below.

Keighley & District bought 15 TransBus Mini Pointer Darts in 2004. Most had gone 17 years later, but smartly presented 720 (YJ04 LYF) was still at work in July 2021, making its way through Embsay bound for Skipton on a DalesBus service from Ilkley and Bolton Abbey.

Many operators have helped provide the popular DalesBus services over the years. Arriva North East 1604, a Wright StreetLite Max, was in Swaledale in August 2021, passing Buttertubs Road End as it entered the village of Thwaite, working service 831 from Middlesbrough. It would perform a double run to Keld (Tan Hill Road End), the terminus of service 30 from Richmond, run by United for many years following acquisition of the route from Percival's, before climbing the spectacular Buttertubs Pass to reach the market town of Hawes.

Cumbria Classic Coaches ran a Tuesday market day route to Hawes for many years using one of its heritage fleet. Among these was former Crosville Bristol Lodekka 627 HFM, its ECW body convertible to open-top, photographed on the sunny morning of April 19, 2011 when it was approaching Ais Gill, which at 1,169ft (356m) is the highest point on the Settle & Carlisle railway. Ninety-eight years earlier, in September 1913, 16 passengers died and 38 were injured in a tragic rail accident here.

Hodgson's of Barnard Castle operates tendered services for North Yorkshire County Council. A rare surviving example of a market day service is the 73 providing northern Teesdale communities with a Wednesday bus to Barnard Castle. Optare Solo YDZ 533 was departing the northern terminus at the Langdon Beck Hotel on the middle of the three trips on July 28, 2021.

The attractive and peaceful village of Kirk Yetholm in southern Scotland marks the northern end of the Pennine Way, a welcome sight for those who have walked the route from Edale. The village has a bus link to Kelso, currently provided by Peter Hogg of Jedburgh. Optare Solo SR YJ13 HJA sets off from the cobbled square in Kelso in August 2021.

A **Grand** Day Out...

CHRIS DREW tells the stories behind eight pictures he took on memorable trips away from home...one involving a skeleton and another an orchestra's many and varied instruments

...with a view from a Cunarder

The seat I was lounging in had been shaped and sculpted by 10 years of use by Glaswegians' backsides. I had found it on the top deck of an exhibit at the Museum of Transport in Clapham.

Out of the window was a throng of humanity getting to grips with all this history. The ambience was one of affection, a far cry from the sterile atmosphere that many museums portray. Apart from B430 (centre stage) and the precious royal carriages, the public could access just about everything, even have picnics on the buses. From all directions, one overheard voices talking about how they had driven one of those or used to go to school or work on that.

I could have propped my trusty Agfa Isolett against the glass at any point in the day and come away with a similar photograph. It was taken and I sat back, grateful to the good burghers of Glasgow that they had the bravery to carry on with trams as long as they did along with other thoughts such as, mmm, wonder what a Cunarder might have looked like in red and cream working London's rails? That 1952 tram was probably the most modern item in the museum.

After nationalisation in 1948, the London Transport exhibits were collected together with those of the other nationalised industries, the railways and waterways, so they would be collated and catalogued under the umbrella of a newly formed Department of Historic Relics.

By 1952 a site had become available. It was the just closed tram depot in Clapham High Street. It was to be used as a store with visits by appointment only. There were small exhibitions held but it was not until 1963 that the paying public was allowed to see the wonders within.

After the BTC was abolished in 1962, the various new boards took back their exhibits. The Waterways Board put together a new museum in Stoke Bruerne near Rugby. The British Railways Board moved lock, stock and piston rods to the National Railway Museum in York and London Transport's exhibits took up a temporary home at Syon Park until a permanent home was found for it at Covent Garden in March 1980. This is where I cannot help feeling that there was a move back to that sterile feel that Clapham had got away from and is more aloof, and consequently, less interesting for it.

As for the Cunarder, tram 1392, it returned to Glasgow and is in the Riverside Museum where it is the focus of a display about 1950s ballroom dancing in the city. More memories.

...on the Epsom Downs

It is the transport event that cannot be found on any rally calendar yet it is something that every enthusiast has to sample at least once, well twice maybe, just to prove it was not simply a dream. When I first started going in my teens, the noise of it all was almost overwhelming.

At that time the Derby used to be held on a Wednesday which meant bunking off school. My parents, bless them, knowing what the day meant to me would offer to phone my school with a reason for my non-attendance that day, not the fact that I had gone horse racing, of course.

At the beginning, it meant an early start, catching a bus to Kingston and hoping to connect with an exotic green 406 which would deliver me either to the Downs if it was going to Tattenham Corner station or more often Epsom High Street, which meant a walk. The upside of that scenario did offer the chance of photographing vehicles heading up to the course.

Once on the Downs, the enormity of the subject hits home. I can clearly remember on the first occasion being staggered by just how many buses and coaches there were and that they came at me from so many angles. And what stuff it was. The open-toppers were guided to places along the finish straight where they were used as makeshift grandstands by those who had hired them while bookmakers set up their pitch in front of them.

Up on 'The Hill', earlier arrivals grabbed a space to set up picnic tables and start up their barbeques. From up there, you could pass an eye along the lines of open-toppers; invariably almost every region of the country was represented by them. It is a timeless scene and it would not really matter what coach was in the shot.

Every time I look at this photograph, I am transported back to the race meeting on Epsom Downs and the ear-shattering roar that emanates from the long stand as two horses battle it out, stride for stride, neck and neck up the straight to the finishing post. I say it would not really matter what coach it was, but I am glad it was this East Kent Leyland Leopard with Duple Dominant body.

...and McGonagall liked it too

Beautiful city of Edinburgh! the truth is to express,
Your beauties are matchless I must confess,
And which no one gainsay,
But that you are the, grandest city in Scotland at the
present day!

These are the last four lines of a 39-line, one-verse epic poem by William Topaz McGonagall called *Beautiful City of Edinburgh*. He described Scotland's capital city with his own inimitable style of unruly scansion (and punctuation) leaving one breathless.

He was right, though. Edinburgh is a beautiful city and all credit must go to its occupants for keeping it so. The Grand Day Out in question started the previous evening when I boarded the overnight coach from London Victoria.

I had been invited to see the Military Tattoo by a friend who was at the university medical school. I was offered a ticket and a place to stay in return for transporting a skeleton in a suitcase. Before you ask, it was not real but it was hers and the studies had moved on to a point where it was needed, so I obliged.

I carried the suitcase around with me while I took photographs and I suppose I was a little disappointed but mostly relieved not to get stopped by McLevy, Inspector of Police, with my companion in the bag.

Together we did the tourist trail taking in the elegant Georgian streets, squares and crescents of the New Town, designed and laid out by the 26-year-old architect, James Craig. We stood on Waverley Bridge and looked at the medieval Old Town which straddles the ridge running from the castle to Holyrood House

Finally, I lugged this literally deadweight up to the castle where I met not only my friend but also an Eastern Scottish Alexander-bodied Bedford YRQ coach which had done the tour the easy way. This was a time before hop-on/hop-off open-top double-deckers did that kind of thing.

A grand photographic day was had by me, a very noisy evening was spent at the Tattoo and after catching up on lost sleep, I said goodbye to my friend and her emaciated workmate and spent the next day in Glasgow about which McGonagall had written an equally tortuous poem.

...by the river

Anything up to a quarter of a million people will line the banks of the River Thames between Putney and Mortlake on University Boat Race day. If you add to that the worldwide audience of an estimated 100million, then as sporting events go, the Oxford and Cambridge boat race is, as they say, right up there.

The origins of the race go back to 1829, the same year George Shillibeer started his first omnibus route in London. It became an annual event from 1856 and apart from the two world wars and 2020, the pandemic, it has never missed a year.

This was not my usual boat race day out. Friends were going to ring a quarter peal at St Mary's on the Putney side of the bridge and as long as I got there before they started, I was going to be allowed on the tower roof to take some photographs. There was a certain irony about the position where I was standing. Had it been 30 years before, I would have had great view overlooking the entrance to Putney Bridge garage, but for now, my interest was held by the traffic in the opposite direction.

There were sightlines across the bridge, up the river towards Fulham football ground, Putney High Street and the Lower Richmond Road. Many years later, someone with better eyesight than me pointed out that in one of the Lower Richmond Road shots, there was a man with a stripey jumper and bobble hat, in the crowd just like in the books where you look for a man who, for copyright reasons, cannot be named. I will not make you search too hard but he is by the bus shelter.

In that moment of recognition by a person much younger than me, the emphasis of the picture changed from being one about the armada pursuing the boat race crews heading away in the distance to one that made my small son very happy, and I had not seen it.

By the way, for those who wish to know, St Mary's is an eight-bell tower and the tenor weighs in at 15cwt. And just to add a personal note, the tower moves somewhat alarmingly when the bells are swinging.

...for a kid in a sweet shop

If you were a fan of London Transport, 1983 was a bumper year, its golden jubilee when it made the most of the public relations opportunity that presented itself.

Various open days and special rallies were held around London, but possibly the *crème de la crème* was when the doors were flung wide at the Aldenham bus overhaul works on the edge of Hertfordshire. On a lucky day, it might have been possible to creep into a garage without anybody noticing, but this could never have happened at Aldenham. Almost the only view one got was from the top deck of a 107 bus.

Of course there are exceptions. In my very young days, my next door neighbour Jim Cobb worked as a bus driver at Mortlake garage. He was also the captain of the garage cricket club and as such would take the team along with friends and family members to tournaments with other garages. A large grass field situated at Aldenham was where the matches were held.

As a group, quite early on a Sunday morning, we would all get on the bus at Mortlake. It had many of the characteristics of a works outing, with singing emanating from upstairs. On several occasions when the match stopped for lunch, Jim would show us around parts of the works ,and as it was Sunday, all was silent, which in the huge place it was, made it feel very eerie.

The particular open-day morning in September 1983 dawned fair. The trip was easy, Underground to Stanmore then a fleet of show buses from various garages ferried the crowds up and over Brockley Hill and in through the gates made famous to all in the film *Summer Holiday*.

From that point on, it was like being a kid in a sweet shop. The new panels can be seen on the body of RM1341 as it levitates above a set of running units which had been overhauled.

...if unexpected

I was asked one day if I could make myself free for ten days' work the following summer. As it was a tour of Switzerland with the youth orchestra, I made a joke about getting my secretary to check my social diary, then I jumped at it.

For several years I had held the title of logistics manager for any tours, gigs etc. This boiled down to getting instruments and equipment from A to B on time and ready to be set up to start a concert.

The tour was to be centred on the Swiss village of Tiefencastel. This would mean loading up the Sprinter with everything orchestral from triangle to timpani and, of course, Tubular Bells. That would be followed by a 12hr drive split by an overnight stop.

Strasbourg was chosen on the way out. This was a shame because it meant some tram photography would have to be attempted, but that is for another story. Similarly, the last show of the tour was set for Basel on the way home. Even more trams. What is a boy to do?

The tour took in four other venues in six days — Chur, Davos (where the members of the orchestra took the train and the coaches and I followed over the hills), St Moritz and Tirano just across the Italian border. I liked the look of Chur (pronounced Coor) and when I realised I was not needed for a whole day while the rest went sightseeing, I bought myself the equivalent of a one-day travelcard which gave me free reign on the Rhaetian railway and Postbuses.

The town is the major transport hub of the area. Not only is it the meeting point for the narrow gauge mountain railway but also the standard gauge railway, which links to most other parts of Europe. Then there is the Swiss Postbus, and the municipal ChurBus services as well.

The PostBus terminal has to be seen to be believed. It looks to be the size of a football pitch and has a clear glass dome over the top of it. For those not so interested in the transport, the 800-year-old cathedral is well worth a look.

I took the train down to Chur about 35km to the north-east in the Grisonian Rhine Valley, taking just over the half hour to complete the journey. Just before the train enters Chur, it becomes a tram with the line running down the main road to arrive at the Bahnhof which is at street level.

After a warm day's photography, sightseeing and, because I was not driving, trying a few local beers, I decided that for my transport back I would try the 182 bus which went up and over through the mountain villages and dropped me back to Tiefencastel Bahnhof an hour after showing my pass. My driver told me then that he never got tired of the views and I could understand why.

My ride was this Iveco Crossway seen leaving again for its return to Chur, just giving me time to dash across the road to take the shot. I also gained a respect for Swiss bus drivers along the way. ■

Greater Manchester PTE 336 (NJA 336H), a Bristol RELL6G with Alexander Y-type bodywork, was one of 30 purchased by North Western in 1969 before the company's division, with all 30 passing to Selnec PTE in 1972. This was August 11, 1978 in the extreme north-west of Derbyshire in the village of Padfield between Glossop and Hadfield in Longdendale, a beautiful area better known for the passage of the Woodhead railway line from Manchester to Sheffield which was, indeed, the reason for my visit. Having walked 15 miles from Dunford Bridge, on hearing the approach of a bus I decided to photograph it, whatever came, a classic "grab" shot.

Days out in Derbyshire

JOHN WHITEING provides a pictorial selection of vehicles to be found on a cross-section of urban and rural services in Derbyshire, some of them provided by operators based in surrounding counties

D erbyshire is a county of contrasts: moorland in the north, the Peak District in the west, a flatter landscape in the east as the land levels out towards the Lincolnshire fens and a southern extension into the Midlands plain.

The county comes within a dozen miles of Manchester in its north-western corner, within half-a-dozen miles of Sheffield city centre in its north-eastern corner and near enough the West Midlands in its south-west for the proximity to be redolent in the local accent.

The towns, for the county is blessed with no large settlements other than Derby (which became a city in 1977 during the Queen's Silver Jubilee year) and Chesterfield, reflect these contrasts in their appearance; stone buildings predominate in the north and west but brick is favoured in the more industrial and former coal-mining areas in the east and south of the county.

Bus services reflect these contrasts, with high-frequency urban services in areas such as Derby and Chesterfield (the only ones that had municipal buses), and rural low-frequency services in the north and west. Trent and East Midland were the two National Bus Company subsidiaries in the county.

Derbyshire County Council's County Bus unit and the Peak Park Planning Board were pro-active in the provision of bus services, the latter especially with the needs of the day-tripper in mind.

Consequently, services were quite significant on Sundays and bank holidays to cater for such requirements, although some of this provision appeared to lack a degree of logic, with some rather unexpected operators providing local services.

So enjoy this visit to Derbyshire, spanning 31 years from 1978 to 2009, and marvel at the variety which existed until relatively recently. By way of example, as well as the more obvious native operators, at various periods it was possible to travel between Matlock and Matlock Bath on buses operated by Maynes, Yorkshire Rider, Yorkshire Traction and, perhaps most surprisingly, Rossendale. ∎

ABOVE: *Chesterfield Transport had a penchant for the Leyland Panther and 11 (NAK 511H), in Elder Way on July 19, 1982, was one of five with Marshall dual-doorway bodywork acquired from West Yorkshire PTE in 1975 and new to Bradford in 1969. As well as buying two batches new, it acquired further used Panthers from Merseyside PTE in 1977/78. Behind, operating the 200 service to Sheffield, is South Yorkshire PTE Series B Leyland National 1066 (AKU 166T), the last of eight new in 1979 which were delivered in National Bus Company leaf green to expedite delivery during a period of vehicle shortage.*

LEFT: *This was Derby City Transport 104 (GTO 104V), a Marshall-bodied Dennis Dominator, in Corn Market in the city centre on the 159 Normanton Lane service. It was one of three Dominators new in 1980 and exported to Hong Kong in 1986. Derby's other three Dominators, new in 1981 with Northern Counties bodies, were sold to Thamesdown in 1986 in exchange for ex-London DMS-class Fleetlines, a type that Derby first acquired in 1979.*

RIGHT: *Silver Service acquired 68 (LHG 386H) in 1982. It was a Bristol RESL with Northern Counties body new to Burnley, Colne & Nelson in 1970. It was at Fairholmes beside the Derwent Dam on July 10, 1983, operating the car park/main road shuttle, illustrating the provision of bus services on Sundays for day-trippers and so often provided by an operator based some distance from its usual areas of operation. The Derwent Reservoirs lie at the eastern foot of the Snake Pass in northern Derbyshire, but Silver Service was based in Darley Dale, near Matlock. Note the Sheffield City Transport bus stop.*

During the summer season of 1984 the 17 service from Chesterfield to Matlock was extended on Sundays and bank holidays to terminate at the Tramway Museum at Crich where East Midland ECW-bodied Leyland Olympian 311 (SHE 311Y), new in 1982, was waiting on July 8.

This similar ECW-bodied Olympian was also at Crich, presenting another example of an operator providing services well beyond its usual area. Yorkshire Traction 672 (C672 GET), new in December 1985, was in the quarry car park at the Tramway Museum on April 30, 1995, between journeys on the marathon 4½hr 901 service from Huddersfield, starting at Tracky's Waterloo depot and serving every stop, all the way. Through passengers were rare, but intermediate usage was quite reasonable. This bus had started life with high-backed seats for limited stop services, but they had been replaced by then following an over-zealous celebration of Guy Fawkes night by college students. The replacement seats came from similar Olympian 666 which had lost a battle with a low railway bridge in Huddersfield. However, 672 retained its high-ratio rear axle which meant it could maintain a good speed on the 901.

Leaving Derby bus station for Swadlincote, in the south-western corner of the county on May 1, 1990 — almost four years into deregulation — is former London Transport DMS1991, Leyland Fleetline 551 (KUC 991P) and one of two acquired from South Wales Transport in 1986, both having their Leyland O.680 engines replaced with Gardner ones before entering service. Its MCW body has been rebuilt seamlessly to single-doorway configuration; earlier conversions with some other operators used an untidy tell-tale smaller window where the centre exit had been. Note the destination display which, on both buses, appeared to have originated in Leyland Nationals, with the characteristic rounded top edge. Trent's attractive post-deregulation livery suits the bus admirably. Having purchased Fleetlines as early as 1963, Trent clearly had a greater admiration for their qualities than London Transport. Both DMSs were withdrawn two months later, in July 1990.

Also in Derby bus station on the same day was this example of the post-deregulation competition that Derby City Transport faced from Nottingham-based Camms, which used the slogan Catcha Camms. Its 159 (LDC 78P), a Northern Counties-bodied Daimler Fleetline, was new to Cleveland Transit in 1976. Camms later changed strategy, concentrating on contracts such as schools and works services, with Derby taking over the competitive operation in the spring of 1993, even painting some of its own buses cream and orange with Camms fleetnames.

Felix Bus Services, based in Stanley, operated into Derby from Ilkeston on a long-standing service which latterly was marketed as the Black Cat. Purchased new in December 2001, Plaxton Pointer-bodied Dennis Dart SLF X711 GJU was on the Felix stand in Derby bus station on June 4, 2002, loading for a journey to Ilkeston Hospital. Ten years later, in 2012, the Wellglade Group, owner of Trent Barton, took over the bus operations of Felix.

Within the magnificent grounds of Chatsworth House on September 20, 2009 while operating the hourly 215 service between Sheffield and Matlock was TM Travel YT55 TMT, an East Lancs Myllennium-bodied Alexander Dennis Dart new in 2005. It was passing Sheffield-bound YN06 CYO, a Plaxton Centro-bodied VDL SB120 new in 2006. Wellglade acquired TM Travel in January 2010.

Another long-established Derbyshire operator, which still operates today and celebrated its centenary in April 2021, is Hulleys, based in Baslow. In Bakewell on April 19, 2004, operating the 170 service to Chesterfield, was 14 (M803 PRA), a relatively-rare MAN 11.190-based Optare Vecta, new to Trent in 1994.

Also in Bakewell square on the same date is Rossendale Volvo B7RLE 151 (PO53 OBM) with Wright Eclipse Urban body and new in September 2003. Although branded for service 464 (Rochdale-Accrington), it was operating another of the marathon Sunday/bank holiday services, in this case from Rochdale to Crich Tramway Museum. The service was split into three to comply with domestic drivers' hours rules. It was about to head south on the third and final of these services, the 473 to Crich; earlier legs were from Rochdale to Glossop and from there to Bakewell. During the high summer of 2005, I travelled on this service between Chatsworth and Glossop via the Snake Pass and was the solitary passenger throughout, despite it being a magnificently fine day. It did not operate in subsequent seasons.

A West Yorkshire Road Car Tilling Stevens B10A of 1929 with a vertically-hinged metal bible destination board in a flimsy unilluminated frame. KEITH JENKINSON COLLECTION

The **lost art** of **bible boards**

As **KEITH JENKINSON** explains, two territorial bus companies swam against the tide by adopting old technology to tell passengers where a service was going

The electronic destination displays that grace most modern buses outside London are a recent development and are simply the latest development to have evolved over the past 120 years of motorbus operation from simple wooden boards to single roller blinds, twin blinds showing the final destination and intermediate points, and multiple apertures with separate route numbers.

By the 1920s, London General and many of the capital's pirate operators used a combination of wooden intermediate destination boards and a roller blind for final destination, or stencil for the route number, before eventually abandoning the wooden boards for roller blinds.

Curiously, by the start of the next decade two major Tilling & British Automobile Traction (TBAT) companies – Eastern Counties Omnibus Company and West Yorkshire Road Car Company — did the opposite and abandoned roller blinds in favour of steel destination boards. These were known colloquially as 'bibles' because they had page-type leaves which opened like a book.

The Eastern Counties bible board and spotlight system on an Associated Daimler 425. JF HIGHAM

Different shapes and lights

Although both companies used basically the same type of bible board, they differed in the method in which they were lit. Eastern Counties preferred uncovered spot lights, while West Yorkshire chose normal light bulbs hidden behind shields.

The shape of their heavy metal boards also differed, with Eastern Counties' being rectangular with a horizontal hinge, while West Yorkshire's had a slightly arched top and initially a vertical hinge, making them look even more like a book; this was changed to a horizontal hinge in the mid-1930s.

Dependent on the number of leaves, the maximum usually being two, the weight of the board, which measured 39in x 18in, was quite considerable and they were difficult to lift to the mount located above the windscreen.

Bible destinations were only used at the front of buses, however, with route details on their sides and rear, where fitted, usually on wooden boards mounted on the roof of single-deckers or below the lower deck windows on double-deckers.

West Yorkshire adopted the bible destination as a standard fitting around 1928 when its Tilling Stevens buses and Leyland Titan TD1s, delivered new with roller blind destinations, had their apertures covered over with frames to

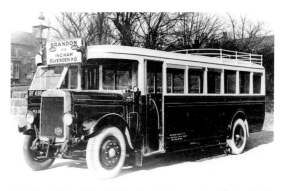

A Leyland Tiger TS2 with Leyland body, new to Midland Red in September 1928 and acquired by West Yorkshire in June 1930. For reasons not known, it was photographed equipped with Eastern Counties' bible boards and spot lamps to illuminate them. KEITH JENKINSON COLLECTION

accommodate the new metal boards. At first these were nothing more than hollow metal frames with no backing, but after finding these to be flimsy and easily distorted, a steel plate was inserted to keep them in shape.

The destination board itself was held into position with strong spring claws mounted at each side, and these also required physical strength to open and close, and as routes were altered, the boards needed to be repainted to show the new details.

The conductor is struggling to turn over the heavy horizontally-hinged leaf on one of the last buses purchased by West Yorkshire with a bible destination. It was an ECW-bodied Bristol L5G new in 1941. RF MACK

Downsides of boards

One of the many other downsides of bible boards was that when a bus was operated on more than a couple of routes, a second board was required, and this was often carried on the luggage racks of single-deckers and beneath the stairs on double-deckers. That was the official procedure, but in practice it was often slid externally between the nearside front wing and bonnet side, its weight largely preventing it from slipping on to the road.

To accommodate short workings or infrequent journeys, a detachable back board was produced on to which two brackets were fixed to enable a wooden board showing the final destination to be slipped in, this eliminating the need for a full-size hinged board to be used, but soon after the end of World War Two, this was replaced by a metal H-shaped board which could be clipped behind the claws to eliminate the need for the additional back board.

The last West Yorkshire buses to be fitted new with bible destinations entered service in 1941 and all those that followed were equipped with standard Tilling-style roller blind screens. Indeed, when some of the company's Bristol JO5Gs were refurbished by ECW in 1946/47, their bible boards were replaced by roller blinds, as ultimately too

This West Yorkshire 1937 ECW-bodied Bristol JO5G in the West Yorkshire fleet was equipped with an H-board on its destination aperture and is carrying a bible board from a previous journey between its front mudguard and bonnet side. RF MACK

were the 1944/45 K5Gs when they were fitted with prewar ECW bodies in 1950. The same happened to some of the York-West Yorkshire prewar highbridge K5Gs in 1954, before they were given new bodies a couple of years later.

The era of bible destination displays ended in September 1958 when West Yorkshire withdrew its final prewar Bristol L5Gs. Eastern Counties had abandoned them a few years earlier. ∎

A 1937 ECW-bodied Bristol K5G in the West Yorkshire fleet showing the manner in which bible boards were fitted on double-deckers. JF HIGHAM